Past Lives
The Key To Your
Present Relationships

Introducing The Youngs'
Past Life Regression Technique

Two pioneers in the field of past life regression counseling share their special technique and the results based on years of research.

By Robert & Loy Young

Edited by Mignonette Pellegrin

Designed & Illustrated by Krista Daehler

Draco Productions and Publications
P.O. Box 27373
Honolulu, Hawaii 96827

(808) 523-1752

Manufactured in the United States of America

ISBN: 0-936121-00-9

Library of Congress Catalog Card Number: 85-73214

First Printing October 1985
Second Printing November 1985
Third Printing February 1986

This book is part of the work of Robert and Loy Young who have developed Dragon Psychology, an applied spiritual philosophy intended to prepare individuals and groups for effective service to humanity in areas of their choice. The material represents conclusions derived from years of observations and research into a systematic approach to personal development--physically, emotionally, mentally and spiritually. The authors make no claim beyond their belief that the benefits and goals of Dragon Psychology can be achieved only by conscious and consistent application of the principles in one's daily life.

Printed in Singapore

DEDICATION

Who you are now is the sum of who you've been in previous lives. This book is dedicated to anyone interested in taking a fascinating journey of self-discovery and to those who we've helped to begin that journey.

AUTHORS' ACKNOWLEDGEMENTS

We would like to acknowledge Mignonette Pellegrin for the splendid job of editing; Krista Daehler for her inspirational art design; Karin Murashige for her patient hours on the word processor and typesetting, Greg Hasler, Roy Cochran and their team, Peter, Alexia and David for completing the marathon task to get the book out on time; to Lucia Capacchione for her editing of our second book and to all those past and present who have supported us in our work and made it all worthwhile.

Robert & Loy

WARNING — DISCLAIMER

This book is designed to facilitate those who would like to learn a unique tool for helping themselves and others deal with certain problems which have failed to respond to traditional counseling therapies. We are by no means prescribing the Youngs' Past Life Regression Technique as a substitute for medical or psychotherapist treatment, nor do we view it as a panacea for all of life's problems.

The purpose of this book is to educate people in the use of the Youngs' Past Life Regression Technique — it is not a prescription. The authors, editor, designer and publisher shall have neither liability nor responsibility to any person or entity with respect to any loss or damage caused or alleged to be caused directly or indirectly by the use of the The Youngs' Past Life Regression Technique.

TABLE OF CONTENTS

Life does not begin with birth into this world or end with death — life is eternal.

PREFACE

We have written this workbook in order to introduce a unique but practical and effective technique for individual growth. This is a step-by-step "how-to" guide for those interested in exploring past life regression counseling as a tool to help themselves and others resolve certain current-life physical, emotional and mental problems for which they can't find any basis in this lifetime. It is a tool for improving your relationship with yourself, with others and with the world.

Past life regression counseling is based on the belief that our current life is but one of many lifetimes. Each lifetime advances us further along our evolutionary path toward immortality. But, as we progress from one lifetime to another, we take along unresolved problems of past lifetimes. The whole purpose for reincarnating is to get another chance to learn the unlearned lessons from past lives.

The effectiveness of the past life regression technique presented here is not based on any specific religious belief in reincarnation. The success of this counseling technique, however, does depend on one's willingness to cooperate during the regression process.

Reincarnation and the law of karma (the law of cause and effect) have been taught for centuries in the East. In fact, our research into the subject shows that these teachings have been the basic tenets of many of the world's great religions and form part of the belief system of much of the world's population, including many of the distinguished thinkers of the Western world. Based on historical sources, including church history, we've concluded that the teachings of reincarnation. have been suppressed in the West for social and political reasons. After all, if we believe ourselves to be the cause and effect of our own lives—if we are responsible for our own destiny, it becomes that much more difficult for us to be controlled by external forces.

However, it is not our intention to prove or disprove reincarnation, but only to expose our readers to the possibilities of a unique and challenging viewpoint that has provided a structure for our understanding of experiences that would otherwise not make any sense to us.

The result of our intensive research and the tremendous success rate we've had over our many years of helping people find relief through past life regression, have convinced us of the validity of reincarnation. Here, we would like to share the knowledge gained and the conclusions we've drawn based on our research. It is our hope that this material on reincarnation will present the reader with the possibility that past life regression may hold the key to resolving certain major physical, emotional and mental problems.

This method of past life regression counseling which does not utilize hypnosis, is a technique used in Dragon Psychology*, a discipline we've designed to teach individuals and groups how to come into balance in this lifetime and acquire virtues by learning the lessons we need to learn in this lifetime— lessons that involve living harmoniously with oneself and with others.

---

*See page 71 for explanation of "Dragon Psychology."

Many more scholarly books have been written about the teachings of reincarnation, and we are happy to see that there are more and more books being published on the subject of life after death and past life regression as a legitimate tool of psychotherapy. When we first started in the field, we were viewed as witches or warlocks. Had we not discovered in our own regressions that we had been teaching others about reincarnation and past lives in several of our own past lives, we might have been discouraged.

What follows are our conclusions based on our research into the teachings of reincarnation and the law of karma (cause and effect) and the practical application of this knowledge for improving people's daily lives today. Of course, we've studied many historical sources and read several Western works on the subject*. However, our primary objective is to present the reader with information based on what we've observed from first-hand experience—from our own past life regressions, and from our clients.

This workbook is divided into three sections: (1) The philosophical basis for past life regression. This section includes the data on the teachings of reincarnation. (2) Past life regression counseling technique. This includes guidelines and codes of conduct for those using our counseling technique, an

---

*For those interested in a deeper knowledge of the theory of reincarnation, we've listed a few books in the bibliography.

explanation of the technique in general, a detailed explanation of each step of the process and a counselor's text. (3) Personal experiences of past life regression clients. This section also includes interviews with past clients and our answers to questions we are often asked.

How to use this Book

We've written this book in a workbook format, because we believe this to be the best way to learn the material. We advise anyone interested in becoming proficient at our past life regression counseling technique to please read the entire book before attempting to practice the technique outlined here.

Then, reread each section and answer the questions. We suggest that you read the section that explains the purpose for each step of the regression process at least three times. Your thorough understanding of the process assures a smooth and successful counseling session for your client. Of course, as with any technique, the more you practice, the more proficient you will become. The same goes for your clients: it appears that the more one is regressed, the more that person comes to trust his or her intuition, and the more details are recalled.

A Word of Caution

Please note that, although we believe that the knowledge of reincarnation provides a tool for personal development, we are by no means promoting past life regression as a panacea for all of our problems. The knowledge gained is useful only to the extent that it can help solve a specific problem. You alone can evaluate the effectiveness of what is presented in this book based on its benefit to you and your clients.

Past Lives

And Your Relationships

Conclusions from More than a Decade of Research on Reincarnation

The concept of reincarnation presented in this book is supported by our personal experiences and observations based on years of research. It matters very little to us if others choose to view reincarnation as science fiction, the product of a well-developed imagination or pure fantasy. We've taken the position that past lives are real, and that they sometimes hold the key to certain personal problems.

Here is our concept of reincarnation:

Reincarnation is neither imposed on us, nor is it meant to be a type of punishment. We came to planet Earth to learn to overcome challenges that we set up for ourselves as a means of evolving to perfection. Each of us has the free will and power to choose when and where to incarnate. We actually decided to incarnate, and even chose the body that would best express our reasons for reincarnating. In other words, it's like going to graduate school to prepare for a profession —we usually have a good idea about what we need to learn, therefore prior to entering graduate school, we must choose all of the right circumstances, including the right school and the right subjects, that will help us acquire the necessary skills..

If one goes into anything with full knowledge of the outcome, there is no game. So before birth, we decided to forget our previous lives in order to learn anew without being influenced by prior knowledge. It's like getting a fresh start. How many times have you said to yourself, "If I just had the chance to start all over, I'd do it differently?" Well, that's exactly what reincarnation is all about. You get the chance to do it all over again, the way you've decided.

There seems to be four main lessons we need to learn on planet Earth in order for us to evolve to perfection. They are associated with the physical, emotional, mental and spiritual selves. Most of us are highly developed in one area, but very limited in the others. For example, we once worked with a blind client who had a very bad respiratory problem, yet she had marvelous control over her emotions. Her mental state was highly evolved, and she was very interested in her spiritual evolution. Obviously, the nature of her lessons in this lifetime had to do with her body.

There is another client who is emotionally balanced—he never says a hateful word. His body is in great shape, too. In fact, he spends most of his time working out, and is very concerned with his health. Mentally, he is not very active. In one of his past lives he was a brilliant politician, but he never took care of his body. He was emotionally unbalanced, usually screaming in order to get his point across. Obviously, during this lifetime, he's chosen lessons related to the physical body.

We've concluded that no one lesson is superior to the other—all four areas of our lives are equally important, and we can create as many lessons as we need to learn in each area. You may want to evaluate your own life to see how you're doing physically, emotionally, mentally and spiritually. This will give you a good idea about what lessons you've chosen for yourself this lifetime.

Reincarnation and Your Relationships.

It appears that during past historical periods, we incarnated on planet Earth to learn the lessons of being individuals. Often, we lived as hermits in caves.

Before reincarnating into each lifetime on planet Earth, we design lessons that help us evolve physically, emotionally, mentally and spiritually.

Obviously, the lesson was for us to grow spiritually by learning about ourselves. During the period we are now in, however, the lessons appear to be concerned with harmonious relationships with others. In other words, it's a time to learn to relate to and live with families and groups harmoniously as a means of expanding spiritually. This is not to suggest that we must lose our individuality. What it means is that we must learn to work together in groups to find solutions to problems facing planet Earth. So, getting along with families and working together with all groups, small or large, is very important.

During this lifetime, if your attention seems to be focused primarily on getting along with partners, family or groups, this will give you some clues. It no longer works to say, "I'm right and you're wrong." It's time to learn how both parties can be right—the "win-win" approach. It is unreal to believe that any one group has all of the answers. There are many paths that will work, and it's time for all groups to work together synergistically—each contributing what it can to solve the problems facing us. Our lesson this time, is cooperation.

This is the time of the "world citizen." We can no longer think in terms of one race being better than the other, or one sex being superior to the other. Most likely, if you picked a female body, all it means is that you needed to express your emotions and develop your intuition. If you picked a male body, then you probably needed to develop your mental awareness and your physical body. Both are equally good lessons. In fact, based on our observations, people are starting to develop both male and female attributes in the same body - - the androgynous type.

We're at a point in time when it is possible for hatred, aggression and separatism to cease. Just think, if all of humanity really understood that we've all lived before in many different bodies, as both sexes, many races, nationalities, etc., it would be pretty hard to hate the other sex or race, or feel so separate from others. How, for example, could any of us go to war against nations, or hate a race which we know we've belonged to in past lives?

Since each historical period has its specific challenges, we seem to choose the time period of our reincarnation based on the lessons we need to learn. If you viewed each century as a giant play that is being acted out on many different stages, then the props become apparent, as do the costumes and the actors' roles.

As each new generation comes to planet Earth, its job is to examine existing beliefs, discarding old unworkable beliefs while keeping beliefs and activities that have benefited humanity. Of course, the role of each generation is also to originate new ideas that will further humanity's progress. So if you don't like something about the period, then you choose a role to play where you can change things. If you like something and want to see it expand, then you pick a role that would allow you to do that.

In summary, changing outdated belief systems is always one of the major activities of any given time period. But in order to help change those beliefs, we have to incarnate into that period and become an actor in the play. We must each choose the proper costume, props and role.

Once we decide the time period and the role we would like to play, the next step is to pick our family members. Often, they're people we've been with before, but with whom we didn't complete the lessons we needed to learn together. Sometimes, however, they are people we've learned to relate to harmoniously in previous lifetimes. This time, the reunion is for the purpose of helping others. In other words, since the reason for reincarnating this time is not to learn personal lessons, we choose to by-pass a family that will present too many challenges.

Besides choosing our immediate family members, we choose to reincarnate in a group that has a similar purpose in this lifetime—people who will help us learn our lessons and help us overcome our challenges.

Reincarnation, then, may be described as a giant Halloween party where each of us turns up in different costumes, hoping not to be recognized. Sometimes it works and we're not recognized for an entire lifetime, but often that doesn't work. We're usually recognized by one of our former acquaintances before the Halloween party is over.

More often than not, we're so anxious to be discovered in spite of our costume, that we continually give clues as to who we are. Try this exercise to see how easily you can pick up the clues: Look into the eyes of everyone you meet and then close your eyes for only a moment and sense the feelings or energy of the other person. You may be surprised to find how familiar a lot of people seem to you; you've known them before. In fact, we've met very few people who we've not known in previous lives. We may have on different costumes in the form of our bodies and different props, including languages, but our soul energy--our essence, remains the same.

Love and Harmony: The Path to Immortality.

As mentioned before, one of the major challenges of this historical period is learning to live harmoniously with each other; first as families, then as groups and nations. The alternative is to destroy everyone around us, ourselves and finally, the planet.

Based on the data we've gotten from our own regressions and by regressing others, our major task here on planet Earth is to learn intelligent love and harmony. That is, we must learn to apply the heart and the mind to achieve harmonious relationships with all of humanity. This is our salvation.

Hatred and attacks do not bring about peace—by hating others, we invite hatred; by attacking others, we invite counterattacks. We believe the saying of "Love conquers all" to be true. Because of the success of the relationship technology we've developed based on the effectiveness of intelligent love and harmony, we believe that everyone can learn to apply a combination of heart and mind to overcome all challenges.

It appears that the first lesson we need to learn for emotional development is to transform all hatred and aggression into love. For mental growth, the lesson is how to turn negativity into positivity. The physical lesson lies in developing a healthy body free from illness and disease. When we've learned all of our lessons on all of these levels, we will have learned to apply love and harmony physically, emotionally and mentally to ourselves and to everyone else. Spiritually, this means that we've broken the birth-death cycle and no longer need to incarnate on planet Earth unless we choose to for reasons other than personal evolution.

What Happens After You've Mastered Harmonious Relationships?

Apart from the beautiful feeling you get from being in love and harmony with everyone and everything, it appears that you get to decide whether you want to help planet Earth evolve by teaching others how to achieve love and harmony. Two examples of people who made this decision, as recorded in the Bible, are Elijah and Jesus. It is believed that many have gone to other planets, and some have assumed the role of teachers to help others on planet Earth.

There are supposedly approximately 65 persons who've broken the birth-death cycle, and are now known as "Ascended Masters," working to help planet Earth evolve. They've completed their lessons of love and harmony, but decided to stay around to help. According to our research, most of the "Ascended Masters" live in the Himalayas in the same bodies they had when they learned the lessons of love and harmony.

Of course, we're not claiming to have regressed any of the "Ascended Masters," so this knowledge is not based on first-hand data. However, we've regressed several persons of wisdom who have accessed this information from their "in between lives"—periods when they have decided not to reincarnate into the physical world. These are well respected teachers in this life, totally dedicated to teaching the virtues of love and harmony.

As stated previously, we believe that mastering love and harmony, or harmonious relationships, is why most of us are here—by choosing to reincarnate, we've given ourselves another opportunity to learn the lessons. We keep giving ourselves the same lessons until we learn them. If you looked at your own life, you'll probably find someone with whom you've had a relationship that didn't end up in love and harmony. Well, according to our research, you're likely to reincarnate with the same person again, not as punishment, but to give yourself the chance to achieve a harmonious relationship. If it isn't the same individual, it will be someone who, in your mind, is very similar.

For example, one of our clients was married to an alcoholic who often beat her up. During a regression session, she discovered that this wasn't the first time she had been with such a person. She'd had three lovers in past lives who fitted this pattern. Also, her father had been an alcoholic who physically abused her when she was a child. It became apparent that she was repeating a pattern in order to give herself an opportunity to learn the lesson of love and harmony. Interestingly, during one regression, this client also contacted a past life in the days of the Vikings when she had been a man who got drunk and beat up women for the sheer pleasure. She finally understood that her reincarnations with alcoholics gave her the opportunity to work out the karma of that lifetime—she felt she had paid her dues. She was able to help her husband get over his problem of alcoholism. Now they are happily married.

We've regressed a great many people who have incarnated to help bring about the "Golden Age"—the age of goodwill, love and harmony. In fact, it is the data from these regressions that have led us to conclude that the major lesson for this age is harmonious relationships. The great majority of these people have incarnated since 1940, and quite a few of them have revealed that there are many more that will be incarnating expressly for this purpose before the end of the century. The number could be somewhere in the millions. Apart from helping those interested in spiritual development, they are incarnating to work in the areas of politics, education, the arts and sciences, business and New Age churches that are universal in outlook.

In conclusion, if our data turns out to be correct, we can look forward to a beautiful future for planet Earth. Our work in past life regression has given us hope for a better world.

Reincarnation Study Section

CONTENT

STUDY SECTION

Reincarnation is like a cosmic Halloween party where past-life acquaintances
may or may not recognize each other.

WHAT IS REINCARNATION?

Reincarnation is the theory that everyone has an immortal soul that incarnates again and again in different physical forms or bodies in order to develop to its maximum potential. Through free will, the soul chooses when and where to incarnate depending on the particular lessons on which the soul chooses to concentrate. In other words, each life is like a blank canvas or raw piece of clay in an artist's hands. The artist (the soul) chooses the medium, with its limitations and its inherent potential for expression, and then expresses himself through the medium.

Each incarnation of the soul has certain predetermined characteristics. For example, the soul chooses nationality, sex, race, physical form (body type), natural endowments (talents) to develop and handicaps to overcome. It chooses the characteristics which will best aid in the lessons or challenges to master. Each life is like going to school to learn lessons we missed.

Before conception, we select the subjects or lessons we need to learn. All knowledge of our previous existences is erased at birth. We get a fresh start—the chance to do things all over again the way we decide.

Reincarnation can be likened to a giant Halloween party at which we turn up in different costumes each time hoping not to be recognized. Sometimes we are not recognized throughout an entire lifetime, but other times we are discovered, especially when we meet individuals with whom we have had powerful past life experiences.

Like repertory company actors, it appears that we travel with the same group of people from lifetime to lifetime. We switch roles and relationships and go from male to female, from parent to child, etc., but the connections continue. Unconscious patterns in our relationships can be repeated from one lifetime to another.

Through the Dragon Psychology* techniques of past life regression counseling, we can uncover deep-seated conflicts and negative patterns of relationships from the past, and then can take the necessary steps to change them into positive ones, based on love and harmony.

*See page 71   for explanation of Dragon Psychology.

STUDY QUESTIONS.

1. What is reincarnation?

2. How does the soul choose where and when to incarnate?

3. Why do we forget our previous existences at birth?

4. Are we the same sex each life?

THE LAW OF CAUSE AND EFFECT.

The law of karma is the principle of cause and effect which is known in the Western world as "every action has a reaction." According to this moral law, if we perform a good deed it will come back to us. The same is true if we do something bad.

Good karma is the result of any action that expresses and fosters love or good effects. Bad karma is generated by any action opposed to love—any action that produces harmful effects. The seeds we have sown in the past (including our past lives) will bear harvest now or in the future. The seeds that we are planting now will affect our future. Love gives rise to love. Thus, if we want to be loved we must love others as we would have them love us.

This ancient teaching is found in the East and the West. It is basic to the notion of taking total responsibility for what we create. We have the power to create our lives as positively as we choose.

The correct use of cause and effect is choosing new, positive actions based on the results of previous effects. Intelligence can be defined as the ability to choose right actions which bring about good effects. If we plan well using intelligence, we get good results. If we don't plan well, we get the results of those actions also, but they may not be to our liking.

Throughout our lifetimes we get countless opportunities to practice our lessons repeatedly until we finally learn that when we cause something, we get a corresponding effect. When we learn this lesson, we become fully accountable for everything in our lives. We keep reincarnating until we get it.

STUDY QUESTIONS.

1. The principle of cause and effect is familiar to the Western world as what concept?

2. What is good karma?

3. What is bad karma?

4. What is the relationship between the law of cause and effect and personal responsibility?

5. What is one possible definition of intelligence?

6. We keep reincarnating until we get what lesson?

GROUP REINCARNATION.

According to Eastern legends, the purpose of our incarnation into the physical plane in the Human Kingdom is to give us the opportunity to advance on our evolution until we reach perfection in this kingdom and evolve into the Immortal Kingdom. There is, however, a much larger aspect to reincarnation: We are all working together to return home to God and we incarnate in as groups in order to do our part of a master plan for evolving consciousness. We choose to reincarnate in a certain group that will facilitate moving planet Earth to the next stage of evolution.

The time when we decide to incarnate and the group we join depends on the type of energy that governs our soul. For example, since Aquarian energy is now coming to planet Earth, Aquarian age souls are responsible for bringing all of the beautiful inspirations of the previous civilization into manifestation. Therefore, many Aquarian age souls are now coming into incarnation to help achieve this purpose of manifesting our new civilization. It is believed that the full blossoming of the Aquarian energy will occur between the years 2000 and 2025. Until the year 2000, we will be busy preparing for this new age.

There are seven types of energy, representing the seven groups into which we can incarnate depending on our purpose in this lifetime. Each group has a different strategy for serving humanity.

1. Pioneers: One of humanity's tasks is to destroy the old, outdated ideas and beliefs of the previous age so

we can build anew. For this reason, souls with the mission of change have incarnated in to help in this project. They are the vanguards, always showing us alternatives to the traditional. This takes people with very special leadership qualities, because change usually is not met with great enthusiasm, but these pioneers are the ones who will lead us to the next step. It is they who will set the direction and purpose for the new civilization through the year 2000.

2. Translators-educators: Groups focusing on education will work closely with the leaders to put the ideas into forms that can be taught to a large public. These are the traditionalists with credentials. Their approach is to teach ideas that work, whether traditional or new.

3. Communicators: Groups of planners will take this information and plan on how to bring the ideas into manifestation through global communication. This group is the marketing experts of ideas. Their approach is to make the planet a global village through communication networks. The current stage of our communication technology would suggest that this group has succeeded in its mission.

4. Creative group: Their task is to add great beauty to the new civilization through the medium of the arts, music, dance, media and other creative endeavors. Their job is to work on the artistic presentation of the material to the mass public through television, books, movies and other mass media. Their approach is to inspire through the arts by irresistibly packaging the ideas for realizing the divine plan for humanity.

5. Scientists-researchers: They must determine what the new civilization should be like. Their approach is to test all new ideas to see if they will work. They are

the test pilots for the pioneers. They are to keep experimenting in order to find the road back home to God.

6. Idealists: The beautiful contribution of the souls of the Piscean age that is now passing out of existence are the visions of peace and brotherhood on Earth. The strategy of this group is to inspire others to the divine plan. They are usually leaders of religious groups.

7. Manifesters: These are the ones who will actually bring about the visions of the Aquarian Age. Since 1975 there have been physical, political and economical upheavals in the world. And by the year 2000 when these are over, we can look forward to magnificent times. The upheavals are a necessary step in bringing in any new civilization because old forms must be destroyed in order to avoid building something new on top of old chaos. We are now in the process of separating the weeds from the flowers or the chaff from the wheat as far as our civilization is concerned. We are learning to discriminate the workable from the unworkable forms. The strategy of the manifesters is to take products and ideas that have been researched and proven and mass produce them for all of humanity. These are usually the people in business.

Although we reincarnate into a group depending on what lessons we have to learn in that lifetime, as we learn our lessons and evolve, we can develop the virtues of the other groups. In fact, we can check our own evolution based on which of these abilities we've acquired. The ultimate goal is to become good at all. But until then, we must work with others with abilities we lack.

This brings us to the subject of group versus

individuals. During Piscean times there was the issue of dependence versus independence. Our purpose then was to learn to stand on our own two feet. During the Aquarian age the focus is on group and universal consciousness. Once we learn to be independent and attain the goal of group consciousness, we will then strive for universal consciousness with all life forms.

Group consciousness can easily be confused with mass consciousness. "Mass consciousness" occurs when a person is still dependent and needs help to survive. Group consciousness is attained by people who have gained independence and can stand on their own two feet. These independent beings then link together to form a group in order to increase their level of effectiveness in achieving their purpose.

In the present day, souls of all energies are responding to the call of the incoming Aquarian energy and are incarnating to bring about group consciousness in all fields of endeavors including government, education, the media, the arts, science, religion and economics. Not only do we work in our individual groups, it is a confirmation of the coming of the Aquarian age to find individuals ready for groups who choose to work together to do their part in bringing in the new civilization and helping the planet evolve.

STUDY QUESTIONS.

1. What is the purpose of our incarnation into the physical plane in the Human Kingdom?

2. Why would we incarnate in as a group?

3. What is the criterion for joining a certain group?

4. What do the Aquarian Age souls have the responsibility of doing?

5. What must be done before we can build a new civilization?

6. List the seven groups into which one can reincarnate depending on one's mission in this lifetime. Describe each group's strategy for helping humanity.

WHAT HAPPENS AFTER I DIE?

This is a question that we've all pondered at one time or another, even if we don't believe in reincarnation. Well, based on our research into spiritual legends from both the East and the West, and past life regressions and reports from individuals who have experienced death, leaving their bodies only to reenter later, the following is our understanding of what happens when one dies. It doesn't matter whether or not you believe the story. What matters is whether it helps you improve the quality of your life today.

It is believed that one does not die without choosing to. Furthermore, there are supposedly seven opportune times for us to leave a lifetime. It becomes appropriate to take advantage of one of those times when, (1) you've completed your mission on planet Earth; (2) you have become so crystallized in your views that you no longer entertain any new views; (3) you become consumed by fear that others will control you. Once you become rigid in your outlook, you invite crippling diseases such as arthritis. So it is right to decide to trade that body in and get a fresh start.

Here is a beautiful picture of what happens when you've decided that it is time to go. If we believe this legend, the thought of death is likely to be less horrifying.

The Welcoming Committee:

A few days prior to death, you're visited in your dreams by loved ones who will be on the other side to greet you. This accounts for the usual reports of dreaming about friends and relations who've died, and also the peaceful look on the face at the moment the person leaves the body. It's a nice thought to know that we'll be welcomed by familiar faces.

Shedding Your Physical Body:

Once you leave your body, as you look back and see your body lying there, the first thought that comes up is, "My God, I'm really not my body!" This is your first realization that your soul and your personality are separate entities. But even with this realization, you may still hover around for 10 days grieving the loss of this piece of possession which you may have been carrying around for a long time. It is believed that cremation after three days releases the soul to begin the task of finding a new body.

Shedding Your Emotional Body:

Although you've discarded your physical body, you're still in a body: the astral or emotional body. You still have an emotional attachment for earthly possessions and relationships. While you are grieving and going through detachment, however, you're in a school—the astral/emotional school where you're taught that you're not your emotional body or your emotions. Until you learn this lesson, you remain in the "ghost" state for a period that can last from a few weeks to thousands of years.

We can help souls to find peace and graduate from the "emotional school" by making sure they make a will, not necessarily a legal will, but just to make sure that everything goes according to their wishes. Furthermore, we can release our own emotional resentments and attachments to them and send loved ones on their way with gratitude saying, "I love you and thank you for the time you spent with me. I'll see you in my dreams."

Shedding Your Mental Body:

When you've learned that you're not your emotions, you take on your mental body and attend classes on the mental plane to examine all of your rigid mental beliefs. You review your problem-solving abilities, your mental strategies and the physical effects of your beliefs. You graduate from the "mental school" when you've learned that you are not your beliefs and let go of them.

Further Journey of the Soul:

Your next stop is on the intuitive plane. Here, your tiny shell of an intuitive body is met by your Guardian Angel, the higher being who has been taking care of you for millions of years. You both review and evaluate your immediate past life to see how it contributed to your evolution. Then, you review the total picture to see how far you've come in your evolution on your way back to God. It is with much joy that you discover that you've come a long way since your first separation from God as a seed sent out to gain experience.

Along with your Guardian Angel, you review how you've learned to work with energy—which virtues you've developed by being able to change negativity into the positive

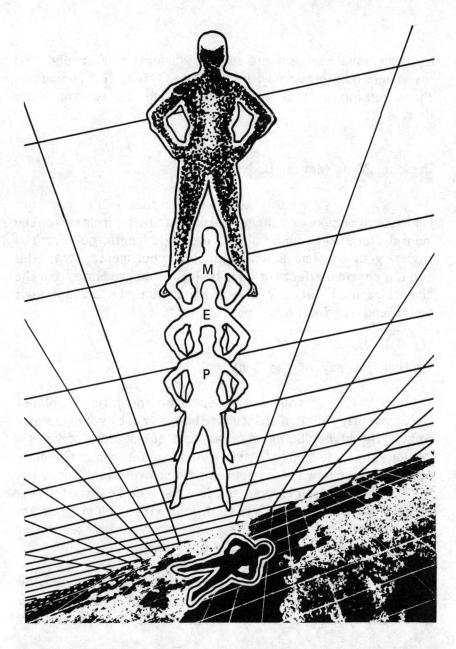

1. The physical body drops away, but the consciousness remains. (The consciousness finds itself out of the body, perhaps floating up above, and observes, with full awareness, what is going on around its deceased corpse.) It would be similar to getting out of a car.

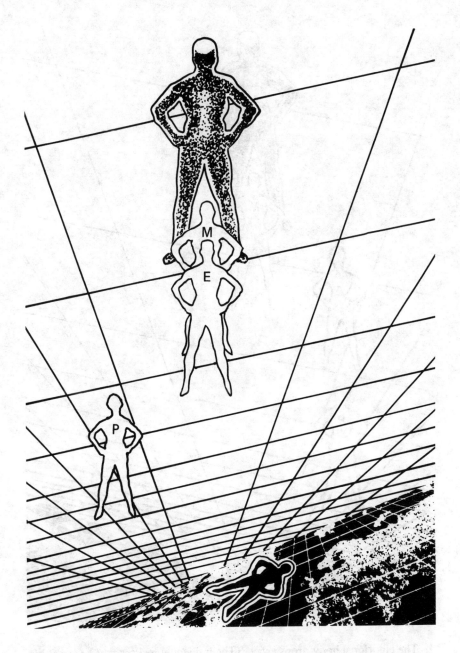

1.a. The car remains behind while you remain fully aware outside of the car.

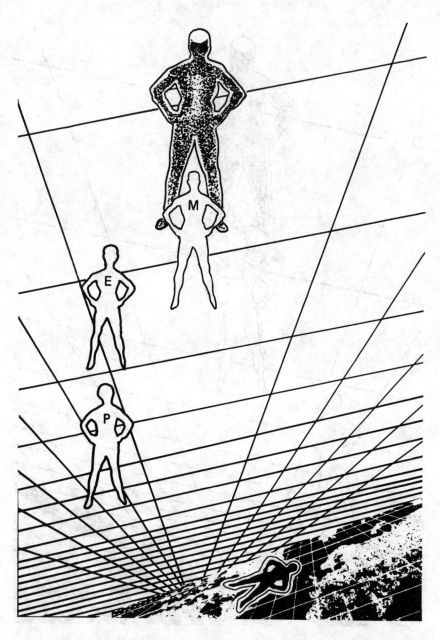

2. The emotional body drops away. (The individual realizes that he is not his emotions.)

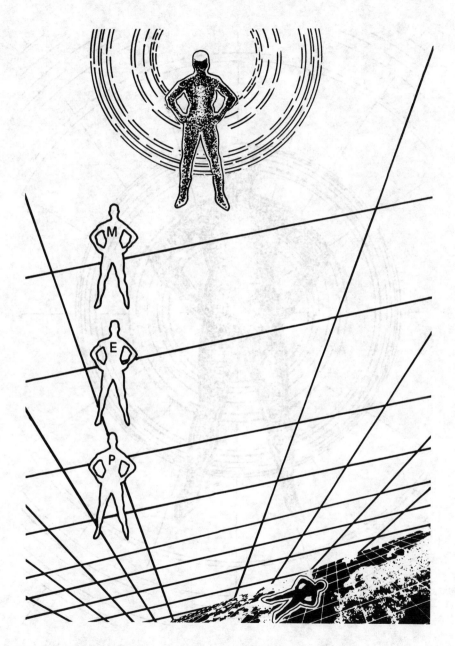

3. The mental body drops away. (Again, the individual discovers that he is not his mental beliefs.)

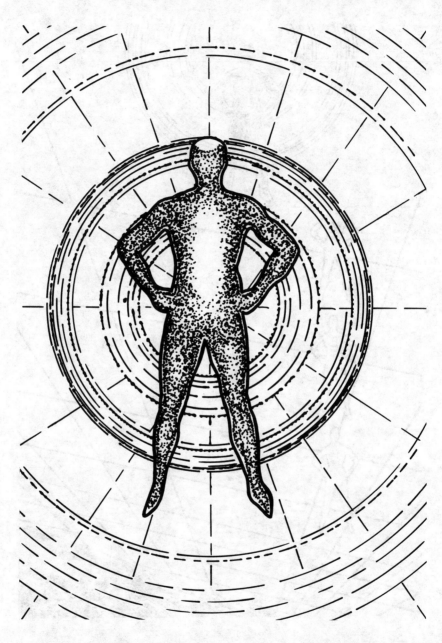

4. The personality meets with the Solar Angel or Inner Guide.

5. Together, they review the most recent life and then all the previous lives. This is a procedure like balancing the books.

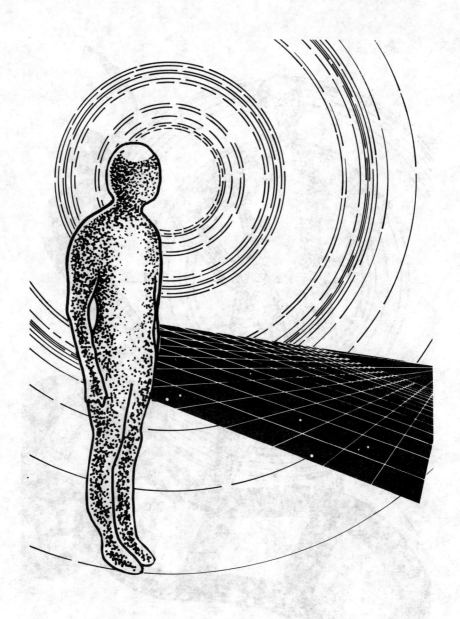

6. Then the individual returns to the Monad (often referred to as the Heavenly Father) to see the Divine Blueprint for the soul's evolution. The original goal or purpose is viewed.

7. Then the individual meets with the Solar Angel again, and the two figure out how best to learn the lessons needed in the next lifetime.

8. The individual again picks up the three elementals or entities (physical, emotional, mental) who build a new body from the point of conception of the fetus.

9. Then the personality enters at the first breath, and a new lifetime and new set of lessons is begun.

use of energy.* The number of virtues you've acquired determines how well you can handle your relationships and how godlike you've become in each lifetime. Sometimes one spends several lifetimes on one virtue—we keep coming back until we get it.

From the Intuitive Plane, your Guardian Angel takes you to the Atmic Plane, that fiery plane where you are totally purified in order to continue your journey.

On the Monadic Plane, you review your personal blueprint to see where you are in your evolving consciousness, and where you are on your path back to God. This is where you get all inspired to keep working on your blueprint.

On the Divine Plane, you review the blueprint for all of humanity. You are fired with the desire to help bring about this plan for humanity, because you can see how you fit into that blueprint.

From the Divine Plane, you retrace your blueprint and readjust it according to the divine plan for humanity. At the Atmic Plane, you further purify yourself. On the Intuitive Plane you develop the desire for service and a "we consciousness;" the desire to work with others. It is from the Intuitive Plane that you reincarnate into a lifetime to do your mission to help bring about the divine plan. The length of time from death to reincarnation depends on how long it takes a soul to go through the various planes.

---

*See page 78 for explanation of energy.

STUDY QUESTIONS

1. How many opportunities do we have to leave a lifetime and when is it appropriate to take advantage of one of those times?

2. Describe the soul's journey from the moment the decision has been made to die to its arrival on the Intuitive Plane.

3. What is the role of our Guardian Angel?

4. Explain what happens on the Atmic, Monadic and Divine planes.

5. From which plane do we reincarnate into a lifetime?

6. What determines the length of period between death and reincarnation?

OUR DEVELOPMENT
FROM CONCEPTION TO 70

Have you ever wished you knew exactly what you were supposed to be doing at each stage of your life? Well, here is one blueprint you might like to consider.

As we mentioned earlier, once we decide to reincarnate, we reenter planet Earth from the Intuitive Plane where we've already figured out what physical, emotional and mental characteristics we need to develop to fulfill our purpose in this lifetime.

According to legend, six months before conception, we choose our parents in a dream state after negotiating about the type of family situations needed for us to learn the lessons we need to learn. Also, according to those lessons, the soul or higher self instructs our physical, emotional and mental selves to create the appropriate personality. The belief is that the circumstances to which we're born indicate our prejudices in past lives. Based on the principle of cause and effect, the circumstances of our present life give us an opportunity to correct the negative effects of the prejudices of our past lives.

At Birth:

It is believed that at the moment of birth, without any consciousness of past lives, the soul makes contact with the body but does not become anchored in the body until age seven.

Our very first lesson, it seems, is to learn

that we're not our physical body and that it is the duty of our soul or higher self to become the trainer of the body. Between ages zero to seven, however, the job of training is taken over by the physical deva (the angel in charge of physical development), because the tendency is for the soul to go in and out of the body during this period. This accounts for why most of us have a difficult time remembering things that happened before age eight. It is a good idea to keep a detailed diary for kids during this time. It may prove useful later in life.

The First 49 Year Cycle:

Ages zero to seven, then, is the time for physical development. It is important that children at this age learn to master the physical body. The emphasis should be on exercises, physical sports, good eating habits and generally caring for the needs of the body.

From seven to 14 is the ideal time for children to learn how to express their emotions in appropriate ways. Parents should take this opportunity to help their children learn how to develop harmonious relationships. This is a great time to teach them the virtues of emotional courage, emotional self-discipline and emotional gracefulness. These virtues allow us to express our feelings, honestly, in ways that do not hurt others. At this age, children must also learn that equality means equal responsibility. This, of course, does not mean that the child must be responsible for everything for which the parent is responsible. What it means is that if the child wants to be treated as an equal and not constantly be told what to do or how to act, he/she must take responsibility for helping the family operate in a harmonious way.

From 14 to 21 is the period of mental development. This is when parents become "know nothings," according to the child's thinking. In some cases, this may be true—many of us parents don't know much about computers or new math or the latest rock music groups. What is important at this stage, however, is that children be taught mental self-discipline—the ability to reason and problem-solve instead of being critical of others.

From 21 to 28 is the time of spiritual development. At this stage the emphasis should be on the importance of service to humanity and development of what we call the "we consciousness." This is the best time to learn to subordinate selfish desires to the needs of the whole family— whether it is our immediate family or the global family of man.

From 28 to 35 is the period of what is called the "fiery will." This is the stage of fierce independence; when the individual sets out "to make a mark for myself." Since this seems to be a period of preparation for something new, it is a good time to plan the rest of one's life based on the cause and effect of what has happened in the past 28 years.

From ages 35 to 42, we usually go in search of our life purpose—the reason we reincarnated. This is when we develop and express our individuality—who we really are. For those of us who are not satisfied with what we're doing at this time, this is a period of restlessness—it is as if we instinctively know that there has to be something more to life. This is when we try to find what that something is.

From 42 to 49 we're usually totally in service, doing what we came here to do; we're in touch with the Divine or the Intuitive Plane from whence we learn the importance of the global family of man and our role in helping to make this planet of ours a beautiful place in which to live. At this stage, we learn to be in harmony with others.

End of the First 49 Year Cycle:

Age 49 is considered a time of completion and rebirth--a new cycle begins. From birth to age 49, at seven-year intervals, we were supposed to have learned our lessons on the physical, emotional, mental and spiritual levels. If we've accomplished this, we can continue to live a beautiful life into later years as we continue to learn based on experiences of the first 49 years. If, however, we've not advanced on the four levels, 49 becomes an age of rigidity. Our flexibility or willingness to learn during each of these periods determines our longevity.

Legend tells us that if someone dies in the second 49-year period, the year in which death occurs corresponds to the stage at which that person became rigid and could not learn what should've been learned at that stage. If, for example, a woman dies at age 65, it is believed that she became crystallized in her beliefs at age 16. At this time of her mental development, she, according to legend, had refused to learn to confront and problem-solve. When she reached that stage the second time and could not work through it, there was an explosion in her physical body which resulted in death. This explosion is usually manifested in terminal illnesses.

The Second 49 Year Cycle:

From ages 49 to 56, we get another

opportunity to learn all of the physical lessons we did not learn in the earlier stages of our development. This is another chance for physical fitness and physical self-discipline.

From 56 to 63, we have another opportunity to resolve all of our emotional and relationship issues. It is a good time to get rid of that one hurt—imagined or real—that one might have been carrying around for years. This is the time to make peace with everyone.

From 63 to 70 is the time to examine all our beliefs and find the ones we've stubbornly held onto even though they no longer work. This is the time to change attitudes such as being critical, judgmental and feeling superior. You might know someone who was very dogmatic in earlier years who, upon arriving at this period, "mellowed out." Those beliefs no longer seem that important.

If, at age 70, you've become crystallized in any of these areas for the second time, it is time to give yourself permission to leave this planet, otherwise you will begin to degenerate physically, emotionally and mentally. Again as we've explained above, rigidity will cause degenerative illnesses.

What happens if you've continued to learn your lessons on the physical, emotional, mental and intuitive levels up to age 70? It is our understanding that you can choose to continue to live for as long as you want. Once you've learned all of your lessons, you have reached the stage of immortality. You can choose to live in whatever form you choose—in the material body, in the spirit or alternating, according to the form that will best help you accomplish whatever you have chosen to do for others who are still working on their lessons.

We've found the above to be an effective blueprint for our own lives. We hope that it will help you make effective use of the opportunity which each stage of life presents. By being aware of this blueprint, you can choose to learn life's lessons with joy. If you are a parent, or someone in the position of influencing the lives of children, we hope that this will give you some guidelines.

STUDY QUESTIONS

1. What happens six months before conception?

2. At what age does the soul finally anchor in the physical body?

3. Outline the stages of development from birth to age 49 and list the importance of each seven-year period.

4. What is the importance of age 49?

5. Outline the stages of the second 49-year cycle and list the importance of each seven-year period.

6. When is it best to decide to leave this lifetime, and why?

HOW DOES A BELIEF
IN REINCARNATION
AFFECT HUMANITY?

It might be a worthwhile exercise to speculate on what would happen if all of humanity believed in the teachings of reincarnation and the law of cause and effect. In our minds, one of the first things that is likely to happen is a reduction in the crime rate. If everyone believed that we will harvest the fruits of our bad deeds either in this or a later lifetime, we would be less likely to do anything that would harm others.

It has been our experience that once people have been regressed and realize that they've been a member of the opposite sex, other races, nationalities, religions, creeds, etc., they tend to be much more tolerant of others.

A belief in reincarnation also appears to give rise to the desire to make the world a better place if we are likely to return to planet Earth, then we have a stake in keeping it healthy and beautiful.

Many of us, if not most of us, live life as if we need to pack it all into one lifetime. With this belief, life becomes a "rat race." We have observed that when our clients become convinced of their past lives and possible future lifetimes, they become much less frantic and are more likely to live in the present; learning the lessons they need to learn in this lifetime.

If the law of cause and effect were to become a popular belief, we believe that the rehabilitation of criminals would become more effective. Prisoners would be taught personal responsibility based on the principle of cause and effect in our view, a far more effective method of changing an individual than just teaching him or her a trade.

Just think what would happen if all of us knew that we have many latent abilities from our past lives, and that all we need to do is access them for use in this lifetime! This may sound far-fetched, but we've succeeded in "reeducating" many of our clients by using a counseling technique which we designed.

A belief in reincarnation might relieve pain and suffering in all areas of our lives. If, for example, we knew that we could find the causes of physical, emotional and mental problems in past lives, we would not have to suffer years of discomfort.

Knowing that we are the sum of who we've been in our many past lifetimes allows for much understanding of ourselves. Furthermore, if we knew that we have a definite purpose in this lifetime, we probably would go in search of our life purpose early, rather than wait to stumble on it later in life. Life is much happier when we know that we have a life purpose which we are fulfilling.

Above all, we believe that if all of humanity accepted the theory of reincarnation and the law of cause and effect, there would be more peace and harmony in the world today. With nothing to lose and so much to gain, we ask that you at least approach these ancient teachings with an open mind.

PART II
The Youngs' Technique
of Past Life Regression

A Reincarnation
Counseling Method
of Dragon Psychology

This section provides the practical application of the teachings of reincarnation. The following is a past life regression process the authors have designed as a tool of personal evolution. It is but one of the tools of Dragon Psychology, a discipline which a group of dedicated professionals have helped research and design as a means of acquiring the virtues necessary for service to humanity.

CONTENT

WHAT IS DRAGON PSYCHOLOGY?

The Symbol of the Dragon

Most of us are familiar with the legends of dragon-slaying. These stories, of course, are based on the belief that dragons are evil. In our context, the dragon represents: 1. a world problem that once solved, moves planet Earth to the next stage of evolution; 2. individuals who have dedicated their lives to serving humanity; 3. one stage of our evolutionary path to immortality through world service.

In the Eastern tradition, especially in Mystery Schools of the East, the dragon symbolizes virtues—the moral excellence that underlies all religions. The main function of these schools is to take the "mystery" out of developing the virtues that will enable us to solve humanity's problems as we evolve into the Immortal Kingdom.

According to legend, the home of the dragon is the constellation Draco, located near the constellation Ursa Major (the Big Dipper). Based on the belief that each of the constellations transmits certain types of energy that help humanity, Draco is believed to transmit energy that trains individuals who have dedicated their lives to serving all forms of life.

As the story goes, those of us who incarnated into this life under the influence of Draco are missionaries sent with the specific purpose of solving a major world problem. So "dragons" are those individuals and groups who recognize that their true life purpose is to make the world a better place, and are ready to develop the necessary virtues. Their path to immortality is through world service.

In Eastern philosophy, the dragon clasping a pearl in one hand is the symbol of the Bodhisattva; the one who returns to serve selflessly. The pearl is the symbol of immortality. When a chosen world problem has been solved, the dragon takes the pearl to the phoenix who symbolizes the Immortal Kingdom. The phoenix accepts the pearl and admits the dragon.

Dragon Psychology, then, is a discipline designed to help individuals develop the virtues we believe to be paramount for world service and for one's own evolution: virtues such as self-discipline, perseverance, the ability to maintain what has been accomplished, courage, honesty and integrity.

Dragon Psychology

The literal meaning of the word "psychology" is "the study of the soul." The word is derived from "psyche" meaning "soul" and "logy" which means "the study of." Dragon Psychology is the study of the evolution of the soul, or the spiritual self, through service to humanity.

According to Dragon legends, in the beginning we were one with God. In order to gain experience in physical reality, we separated from our divine source. Dragon Psychology is a special technology that helps us, on our return home to God, to master the Human Kingdom and evolve to the next kingdom, the Immortal Kingdom.

This is a discipline for individuals and groups who are dedicated to solving world problems. When we dedicate our lives to working for all of humanity, we are said to be under the dragon constellation Draco, which transmits energy for global problem-solving. The methodology of Dragon Psychology is aimed at helping us develop the virtues that enable us to work together to improve life on planet Earth.

Everything is Energy: The Basis of Dragon Psychology.

The underlying principle of Dragon Psychology is that everything is energy. Modern science, too, shows that energy is the common denominator of all matter.

Each of us evolves as a result of learning to use energy to progressively bring about harmonious relationships with ourselves, our family and friends, the groups we belong to, our community, our nation and the world. The ultimate goal of the individual is to use energy positively in world service for world peace.

Dragon Psychology explains the interrelation between the energies of the personality, the soul of the individual and the universe. It shows us how we can use the flow of energy to accelerate our personal growth—energy that comes from sources ranging from cosmic energy to the energy that comes from the food we eat and energy vibrations transmitted to us from others.

According to Dragon Psychology, each individual has four selves: physical, emotional and mental, which make up the personality; and the soul, or the spiritual self. The soul, or the spiritual self which is composed of positive energy, has the task of training the personality to transmute any negativity to the positive. It is through the counseling techniques of Dragon Psychology that individuals develop the virtues for learning to transmute energy. After developing the ability to receive, transmute and use energy positively, the individual is then able to distribute it through service for the benefit of humanity and all forms of life.

In addition to teaching techniques for receiving and transmuting energy, Dragon Psychology has also developed specific techniques for distributing energy in service: how to prepare to be a server and how to further develop previously practiced methods of service. These techniques are employed according to the interests and ability of each individual.

New Awareness

While the precepts, myths and legends of Dragon Psychology may seem strange, it is well to remember that the sole purpose of this discipline is to bring about a new awareness that leads to spiritual growth. Because these concepts and techniques are foreign to the belief systems of most Westerners, some are not sure how to respond to it. A suggested approach to the material is to maintain a sense of open-mindedness as the techniques are utilized and the results analyzed.

STUDY QUESTIONS

1. What does the symbol of the dragon represent?

2. What is Dragon Psychology?

3. Explain the theory of energy that forms the basis of Dragon Psychology.

DRAGON PSYCHOLOGY
COUNSELING

In the field of Dragon Psychology, the purpose of counseling is to help individuals find and achieve their life purpose. Dragon Psychology provides a step-by-step technology to assist people in mastering their personality as the prerequisite for accomplishing their life purpose. The belief is that the more we learn to train our physical, emotional and mental selves, the better able we are to discover and unite with our spiritual or higher self, which then leads us to our life purpose. Until we can attain this self-mastery, we are controlled by our personality, the gratification of whose needs may keep us from achieving our life purpose.

The basis for learning to master the physical, emotional and mental selves is to learn how to master energy. In Dragon Psychology counseling, the aim is to teach people how to transmute energy from negative to positive use. They learn to move through the cycle of energy from inertia to activity to balance, developing virtues while overcoming vices.

In summary, there are three main purposes of Dragon Psychology counseling:

1. To teach people how to train their physical, emotional and mental selves (the personality) as the basis for achieving their life purpose.

2. To teach people how to transmute energy from negative to positive use. In practical terms this means overcoming the vices of the personality by changing them to virtues.

3. To teach people how to move through the cycle of energy,
   from inertia, to activity, to balance.

CYCLES OF ENERGY

            In response to energy and all changes in life,
the physical, emotional and mental parts of us, go through three
cycles: inertia, activity and balance. This is the basic cycle of
action that is normal to any energy or change. When raw energy
is first received, the tendency is for us to resist because we do
not know what to do with the energy. There is a temporary state
of being "overwhelmed" by the energy, so we resist long enough
to try to figure out what is happening. This is when we
experience inactivity, tiredness and sickness and the need to lie
down. This "rest period," or period of inertia, gives us a chance
to figure out what's happening and how to problem-solve. Once
we can problem-solve, we begin to move again.

            The excess energy stored up while we were at
rest in inertia then propels us into activity, taking us beyond the
point of balance into the opposite extreme. The extra energy is
actually needed at first to move us from inertia, but once we're in
full swing we can't slow down. In this phase we frequently are
certain that we have all of the answers, because there is such
pride in breaking the cycle of inertia. If we stay too long in the
state of activity, we can become very crystallized in "my way."
Our way of thinking or doing things becomes the way.

            When the normal cycle of action is followed to
the balance, the energy comes into rhythm and harmony.

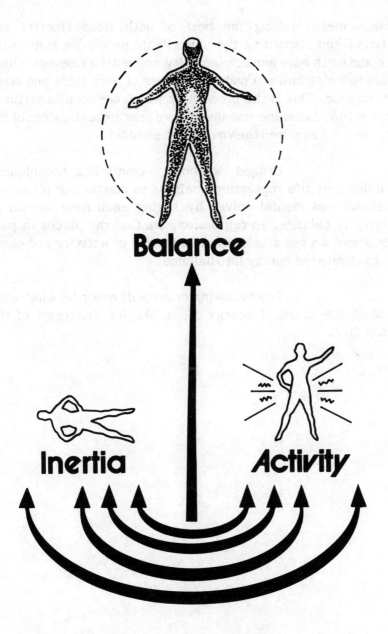

The pendulum swings between the extremes of inertia and activity
until finally we come into balance to enjoy the rhythm and harmony
of the middle path.

Balance means taking the best of both sides (inertia and activity) and discarding the unworkable parts. We may swing back and forth between non-activity and activity several times before learning how to combine the best of both sides and come into balance. This is the process by which we acquire virtues, because to be in balance means to have overcome the vices of the extremes and acquired the virtue of the middle.

Dragon Psychology counseling techniques, including past life regression, help us to master our physical, emotional and mental selves by taking each from inertia to activity to balance. In regression, we find the places in past lives where we got stuck either in inertia or activity and could not transmute the energy into balance.

The following chart will describe what each phase of the cycle of energy looks like for each part of the personality.

MOVING THROUGH THE CYCLES OF ENERGY

PHYSICAL

Inertia

Tired, weak, cannot get out of bed in the morning, no energy, illness. In the most extreme, it is like a "coma" and death.

Activity

Running around, cannot stay still. "Got to go here, got to go there," not knowing where or why we are going, we just have to go. Nervous, sometimes frantic, hyperactive, restless.

Balance

Physically fit, activity to the level that is necessary to achieve the person's life purpose. There are actions and results on the physical plane.

EMOTIONAL

Inertia

Emotional repression, emotionally withdrawn, self-effacing, paranoid, resentful, hurt, sad and depressed, low self-esteem, victim and martyr in relationships.

Activity

Relationships full of emotional dramas, pain and suffering, lots of wants and desires, anger, emotional roller-coaster syndrome.

Balance

Healthy relationships, emotions very calm and stable, articulate, can express love, developed intuitive and creative powers, "we consciousness," into service of self and others.

MENTAL

Inertia

Dull-witted, someone who cannot remember things, cannot problem-solve, blanks out a lot, plays "dumb," nothing works, inflexible.

Activity

Someone who thinks he has all the answers, opinionated, prejudiced, constantly blames and criticizes others because it is always their fault; selfish and egocentric, authoritarian.

Balance

A clear thinker and problem-solver, able to be focused and directed about goals and decisions, carries out plans according to purpose, uses will for the good of the whole.

 The purpose of counseling is to move each part of the personality of an individual from inertia to activity, and then to balance. The counseling techniques vary according to where a person is on this evolutionary scale.

Past life regression counseling is experienced at different levels, depending on where a person is on the cycle of energy. People in inertia will get value out of regression by seeing how they are accountable for their actions, instead of constantly being at the effect of others and the environment. It is usually much safer for those in inertia to accept accountability for something that happened in a distant past life than it is to confront an issue in this life. From this safe and detached place in the past, they can begin to see the value of accountability without feeling guilty. Only if we are accountable for whatever happens in our lives can we make necessary changes.

People in activity would derive a different benefit from past life regression. Whether it is on the physical, emotional or mental level, people in activity experience a great release of stuck energy when the karmic cause, or original past life cause of a current life problem, is discovered. Since those in activity are operating from an overload of energy, this release of trapped energy helps them move toward balance.

THE
DRAGON PSYCHOLOGY
COUNSELOR

A Dragon Psychology counselor is basically a "manipulator" of energy—someone who has learned to transmute energy for positive use, and can teach others how to do the same.

Each of us receives energy. When we receive energy, we must then transmute any negativity to the positive and then transmit the energy, according to our own stage of evolution, to help others.

Servers (those who have dedicated their lives to serving humanity) range from those who have just discovered their life purpose to those who are serving on an international level. The level of service is determined by how much energy they can manipulate or transmute from negative to positive use and then distribute it in service to others. An advanced server is someone who can successfully transmute energy all the way from the negative to the positive use for distribution in service to others.

A counselor is a server who can manipulate or change their negative response to energy to the positive. In other words, a counselor trains others to transmute energy. Usually people go to counselors because they can't transmute energy in a particular area of their life.

TASKS OF A
DRAGON PSYCHOLOGY
COUNSELOR

A Dragon Psychology counselor is an expert at working with, and helping others transmute energy. The counselor helps the individual by:

1. Identifying where the client is on the cycles of energy: inertia, activity or balance.

2. Teaching others to transmute any energy received to its highest potential use, which is developing virtues.

3. Teaching others to utilize the transmuted energy to better their life as well as the lives of those around them.

THE CODE OF A
DRAGON PSYCHOLOGY
COUNSELOR

1. The purpose of counseling is to help others transmute all negativity to the positive and to teach them to transmute that energy to its highest potential.

2. A counselor's duty is to bring those counseled to their own realizations by asking questions.

3. A counselor strives to help clients become accountable for their lives and to confront what is. A counselor does not tell clients what to think or what to do, or support dependency in any manner.

4. A counselor gives support at whatever stage of evolution the clients are in without invalidating their truths or beliefs. The counselor knows that wherever a person is in his or her evolution is perfect, encourages progress to the next level by asking questions aimed at self-discovery.

5. A counselor, being aware that erroneous actions are merely the result of the client's inability to problem-solve correctly, is never critical of the client.

6. A counselor keeps all counseling information absolutely confidential, understanding that such confidentiality is essential to creating a safe environment for the client.

7. If a counselor does not know what to do with a confidential piece of information, or an issue that comes up during counseling, it is the counselor's duty to ask the client's

permission to refer the matter to others who are equipped to handle such issues. The purpose of this is not to destroy any confidentiality, but to deal effectively with whatever comes up for the client.

8. A counselor is in charge of the counseling session and conducts the sessions in a professional manner.

9. A counselor agrees to take full responsibility for conducting the session correctly.

10. A counselor must keep counseling appointments. When appointments are made the client's energy goes into preparation for work at that set time.

11. A counselor maintains enough self-discipline to keep emotions in balance; never negative, always professional.

12. A counselor maintains a safe and pure environment during the counseling session without unnecessary interruptions.

13. A counselor focuses undivided attention on the person being counseled, realizing that this time is to serve the client.

14. A counselor speaks in a harmonious tone of voice without any accusation or judgment.

15. A counselor does not go into agreement with the client's negative perceptions, but understands it was created in some way to further the client's evolution.

16. A counselor knows that there is a good purpose behind every negative action, and helps the client find that good

purpose.

17. A counselor expresses empathy and compassion.

18. A counselor never counsels anyone who is overly tired, as the client's ability to problem-solve is too limited at these times.

19. A counselor, prior to the beginning of the counseling session, helps the client to set very definite goals to be achieved during this counseling session.

20. A counselor ends the counseling only at a point at which energy has been transmuted to the positive.

THE BENEFITS OF
REGRESSION COUNSELING

Past life regression counseling, as presented in this book, is a special technique used in Dragon Psychology to find the root or cause of a specific barrier or blockage of energy, so it can be transmuted. Very often the lessons we are working on in this lifetime are more extensive than meets the eye. The law of cause and effect, or the law of karma, states that you are currently living the effects of seeds that were planted many lifetimes ago—not as a "punishment" or "reward," but simply as opportunities to learn an unfinished lesson. Each soul has lessons that are a special challenge—ones that have taken lifetime upon lifetime to experience both sides of the extremes before developing the ability to choose the balance.

In Dragon Psychology, it is actually preferable for a person to learn to work with the lessons in the context of this life. This is because we are trying to train our physical, emotional and mental aspects to learn the law of cause and effect through present actions, rather than focusing on past mistakes. However, there are issues and lessons we invest a lot of time trying to resolve in the present; no solution seems to work. It's like trying to put together a jigsaw puzzle with half the pieces missing. These are the situations to which past life regression can be appropriately applied.

As in traditional psychotherapy, Dragon Psychology also suggests that an early experience that had a strong physical, emotional, or mental impact on our lives actually shapes our responses and behavior in the present. A frightening or traumatic experience leaves an imprint on the psyche and shapes our beliefs, attitudes, feelings, and even our physical condition. A difference between traditional forms of psychotherapy and Dragon Psychology regression techniques is that psychotherapy deals with a one lifetime framework, whereas in past life counseling the context includes the entire history of previous incarnations.

Both psychotherapy and past life regression counseling recognize that our forgotten (unconscious) past controls our present. Psychotherapy has tools for dealing with the immediate past in our present lifetime, whereas past life regression counseling goes into much deeper levels of the past. Both believe in the possibility of change by becoming conscious of unconscious memories and then changing the negative patterns into more positive ones. By doing so, we take increased responsibility for our lives and gain greater freedom of choice. Both look for the causes of the problems rather than merely focusing on treating the effects.

The purpose of a past life regression is to look at an unsolved lesson in the larger context of a soul's evolution. This is done by locating the original "cause" or karmic cause of the unsolved lesson in the lifetime where an action caused a "reaction" in many lifetimes to follow. Usually in that lifetime, as a result of some action a person took, he made a decision that he is still acting upon today. When one can look at the "cause" lifetime, he is able to see his lesson in a whole new context. With the rest of the pieces of the puzzle in place, the whole picture becomes visible. This sometimes is enough to solve a major problem that has existed through many lifetimes. Once a person sees how he caused whatever happened, it becomes possible for him to transmute the energy in the actual lifetime where it originated, using the knowledge that he now has at his disposal.

When we see how a past life reflects on our

present life, it becomes possible to disconnect from the negative aspects of each past life and create a present and future with a greater sense of freedom and understanding of one's life purpose.

There are some secondary benefits to experiencing regression. First, when we get first-hand experience of our past lives, the concept of reincarnation tends to become a fact based on reality instead of merely an intellectual concept. The fear of death is likely to disappear as we begin to understand that we have countless lifetimes and opportunities to learn our lessons and achieve our purposes.

Second, our prejudices may disappear as we discover that we have been a member of both sexes, and all races, religions, nationalities and personality types.

Finally, experiencing our past life history gives us an opportunity to understand our individual lives within the context of it being one small part of our soul's evolution. We can see how we chose our current lives to learn particular lessons that are needed for the soul's evolution and that we are responsible for the choices that have been made.

STUDY QUESTIONS

1. What is the purpose of counseling in Dragon Psychology?

2. What is the role of the counselor in Dragon Psychology?

3. Explain the "Cycles of Energy" and how it relates to our positive use of energy.

4. List from memory five items from the "Code of the Dragon Counselor." Continue this exercise until you can list all 20.

5. List the similarities and differences between traditional psychotherapy and Dragon Psychology counseling.

6. What are the benefits of regression counseling? List at least five.

Preparation Exercises For Past Life Regression Counseling

CONTENT

PREPARATION EXERCISES

Before doing a regression, it is essential that the person being regressed be properly prepared by getting accustomed to re-experiencing past events through memory. The purpose of the exercises in this chapter is to prepare a person for a regression by taking sequential steps to using memory, opening the senses, learning to distinguish between memory and imagination, and using one's intuition. As we work with memory, we become familiar with just how we remember— whether it is primarily through thoughts, visions, senses, or emotions. Each of us will perceive the past in a different manner.

These preparation exercises are particularly important, because, as we shall explain later, our regression techniques do not rely on hypnosis. Therefore, clients must learn to trust their intuition while in a conscious state.

DIFFERENCE IN RESPONSES

Everyone will respond to these exercises differently. If a person is in inertia,* it may take him quite awhile to do the drills. In fact, you might spend an hour or two on just one drill when the person is in inertia. It is important to take as much time as needed so the individual feels completely comfortable and has really mastered the drills. <u>Do not go on to the next drill or do regression work if there is any doubt or confusion about any of the previous drills.</u>

---

*See page 78 for "Cycles of Energy."

Persons in activity will get through the drills more quickly. They will use action words and will experience the situations more vividly. Although those in activity will move through the drills more rapidly, it is important that the counselor not let them move too quickly. You must help them be observant and not gloss over the remembrance. You really want to be sure that the senses are being used. Ask them to describe the sensory details to you one at a time so you are sure that they are really reliving the experience through all the senses. Help them slow down and be truly perceptive.

Persons in balance usually will have an easy time with all of the drills. They are very observant, methodical, yet quick to understand the drills.

In observing the responses, the counselor should keep in mind that there are different ways of perceiving memory and that each person responds in a way that is natural to him. Some people will have strong perceptions through their emotions and will respond with sadness or joy, for example, whereas others will remember through their senses and have visual memories.

MEMORY VERSUS
IMAGINATION EXERCISES

Purpose: To help a person experience the difference between memory and imagination. Regression work utilizes the memory function; fantasy comes from imagination. A common doubt about the validity of past life regression relates to whether it was real or imaginary.

Exercise #1

Give the following instructions to your client:

1. Close your eyes and remember your last meal. Where were you? What did you eat? Tell me about it.

2. Imagine what you will have for breakfast two weeks from now. Imagine where you might be and what you would be eating. Play with your imagination and make it an unusual situation. Tell me about it.

3. To review the difference between memory and imagination, ask:

   a. How did you experience the memory part?

   b. How did you experience the imaginary creation?

   c. What was the difference between the two?

You might get answers like, "I could remember more details and the facts did not change." Or, "I could recall the taste and smell, but I could not imagine how the food would taste or smell."

Exercise #2

Continue with the following instructions:

1. Select something memorable that happened to you within the last year. Review it in your mind and tell me about it.

2. Now remove the real memory and imagine something that might have happened within the last year, but did not actually occur. Tell me about it.

3. To review the difference between memory and imagination, ask:

   a. Pretend that those were past lives.

   b. How did you experience the memory?

   c. How did you experience the imaginary creation?

   d. What were the differences between the two?

   e. What was the difference in your feelings?

Exercise #3

Continue with the following instructions:

1. Close your eyes. Remember something memorable from your childhood and tell me about it. Erase it when you are finished.

2. Now, imagine something that might have happened in childhood but didn't. Tell me about it. Erase it when you are finished.

3. Review the differences between memory and imagination by asking:

   a. How did you experience the memory?

   b. How did you experience the imaginary creation?

   c. What were the main differences?

   d. What was the difference in your feelings?

Exercise #4

Continue with the following instructions to your client:

1. Close your eyes. Go back as early in your life as you can and recall one of your first memories. Tell me about it. If you are finished, erase the memory.

2. Now, imagine something that might have happened during that same period of time but did not. Tell me about it.

3. Let's review the difference between memory and imagination:

   a. How did you experience the memory?

   b. How did you experience the imaginary creation?

   c. What were the main differences between the two?

   d. What was the difference in your feelings?

In doing these exercises, it's important that the individual understands and recognizes his own emotional reactions to memory. This is a key factor in past life regression experiences.

THE DIFFERENCE BETWEEN MEMORY
AND IMAGINATION

SEQUENCE

Memory
The events appear in a clearly defined sequence.

Imagination
The sequence of events is entirely open since the whole thing is a fabrication of the mind.

DECISIONS

Memory
There are no decisions to make and no questions about what happened as the sequence is a fact.

Imagination
Decision-making is necessary to construct the imaginary event. Imagination has little or no emotional content since it is made up.

EMOTIONS

Memory
Memory has an emotional content. Sometimes the individual becomes very emotional while recalling a significant event from the past.

Imagination
You can manufacture the emotions, but they won't last. They keep falling apart.

RECALL

Memory
Remembered events are always available for recall and they are always the same.

Imagination
Imaginary events have to be made up, and they can be changed at will.

SENSES

Memory
Memory has sensory experience attached to it; sense impressions come up in the recall.

Imagination
Imaginary events tend to be perceived visually. It is a mental process and therefore will not contain the stored sensory memory.

LEFT / RIGHT BRAIN

Memory
Memory is associated with the left brain; linear sequence.

Imagination
Imagination is connected with right brain processing; it is open-ended, unstructured.

STUDY QUESTIONS

1. What is the difference between how people in the energy states of inertia, activity and balance respond to past life regression preparation exercises?

2. In past life regression counseling, why is it important for the clients to be able to tell the difference between memory and imagination?

3. What is the difference between memory and imagination as they relate to:

Sequence _____

Decisions _____

Emotions _____

Recall _____

Senses _____

Left/right
brain
function _____

_____

4. Have someone take you through the "memory vs. imagination" until you are confident you know the difference.

OPENING UP
THE SENSES

Memory is often perceived in flashes or in what photographers call "freeze frames." That means they are unmoving, static and limited. It is important, therefore, to assist people being regressed in opening up their senses in order to perceive memories and past life experiences through all senses. Sense perception greatly aids in opening the memory so the full experience of the past life events can be recalled accurately.

Exercise #1

Give your client the following instructions:

1. Close your eyes.

2. Recall a recent memorable event in your life.

3. Focus on the event you are remembering. Notice the time of day and the setting. Actually be there in as much detail as you can.

4. What was the most distinct taste? What was the most distinct smell? What was the most distinct sound?

5. What was the most distinct texture or object you touched? What was the most distinct picture?

6. What were your emotions at the time?

7. What were you doing? Actually go through your movements and get some activity going in your mind. Walk around and pick things up. Do whatever you did at the time.

8. Now you can open your eyes.

9. Did the memory come more to life as you used your senses? This preparation will help you to experience your past lives fully when you are in a regression. Now erase that memory.

Now, take the person back to three more events in his present life, going back in time in stages, using questions one through nine with each event. Ask them to:

a. Recall a memorable event in your life in school.

b. Recall a memorable event in your life with one of your parents.

c. Recall a memorable event in your early childhood.

STUDY QUESTIONS

1. What is the importance of sense perception in past life regression?

2. What does it mean when we say that memory is perceived in "freeze frames?"

3. Have someone assist you through the exercises for opening up your senses until you are certain you understand the experience.

FINDING YOUR
OWN BODY

The purpose of this drill is to help people locate themselves in the past life, and to accept having been in another body or personality. This may be difficult when there is a sharp contrast between the present life and the past life with which they are working. If, for example, a person leads a very dull, uneventful life, it would be difficult to accept being a person who was very powerful or who was in an active leadership position. On the other hand, it may be equally difficult to contact a lifetime of being ugly, lame, a criminal, or a member of a race or group toward which a person is prejudiced in this life.

It is essential to train clients to be inside their own bodies and not be outside as a distant observer of some scene or situation in which they are involved. Often, when people contact a lifetime in which they were with a famous or charismatic person, they tend to slip into that person's body instead of staying in their own body. This drill helps the clients tell the difference between their body and that of someone else.

Exercise #1

Give the following instructions to your client:

1. Close your eyes and remember coming into this room (today or tonight). Retrace your steps and recall everything you saw, felt and did.

2. Recall the same event, but be me and experience this room from my point of view. Actually be in my body, look out of my eyes, and experience things from my point of view.

3. Now, open your eyes and tell me what the difference was. (Here the client will report the difference in terms of memory and imagination. They know their own viewpoint from memory, but have to imagine your perception.)

Exercise #2

Continue with the following instructions to your client:

1. Close your eyes and tell me what you experience right now about being in this room with me. Tell me what you see out of your own eyes, and what you're feeling, hearing, smelling, etc.

2. Then become me. Visualize that you are me. Enter my point of view, look out of my eyes, and tell me what you experience.

NOTE: What the client will report is that he has to work at figuring out the other person's, in this case your, viewpoint whereas the client's own perspective is easy to describe because it is memory. Trying to figure out another's experience involves imagination.

Exercise #3

Give the following instructions to your client:

The next step is to take the client back to memorable events which he experienced with at least two other people.

1. Recall a memorable event in your life that involved at least two other people.

2. Tell me about it from your personal experience or memory.

3. Now tell me about the experience from the eyes and viewpoint of one of the persons.

4. Tell me again about the experience from the viewpoint of the third person present at the event.

Having clients describe the event from each viewpoint prepares them for getting into their own body, emotions and thoughts when being regressed to a past life. If the clients can observe persons they think they were in a regression, the chances are they are not the persons they are seeing, or for some reason they are not in their body. For instance, all the people who think that they were Napoleon or Cleopatra in past lives might very well have been around Napoleon or Cleopatra. After all, those two people were powerful and came into contact with thousands of people.

Also, sometimes during a regression people will return to a moment in the past life when they were out of the body, such as at the moment of death or during an illness. It is important to get the client to move into the body and look out of his own eyes so he can fully experience the past life personality through all the senses.

The above exercises should be repeated as many times as necessary to train the client to get into the experience of his own viewpoint and physical reality. A client in inertia may take a long time to master this drill. In fact, it could take as many as 20 memorable events from the present lifetime before the client has truly mastered the drill. With a client in activity, less time and fewer repetitions of the drill are needed.

STUDY QUESTIONS

1. Why is it important to have a person learn to be in his or her own body during regression?

2. Why is it sometimes difficult for someone to be in his or her own body after contacting a lifetime?

3. How can you tell whether a person is in his or her own body when describing a past life episode?

4. Have someone assist you through these exercises until you know the process.

INTUITION VERSUS
LOGIC VERSUS
EMOTIONS

There are at least three ways to know something: 1) through logic and mental reasoning; 2) through emotions; or 3) through intuition. By training clients to understand the difference, we prepare them for the regression process. This automatically develops and trains the right hemisphere of the brain (the intuitive, creative processes) and enhances the individual's natural creative abilities.

Note that much of the past life regression process is based on intuition. So it is important that the client's intuitive senses are developed.

Exercise #1

Give the following instructions to your client:

1. In your experience, what is the difference between intuition, emotion and logic? (Listen carefully to the answer and help the client if there is any confusion. Be sure the client understands that intuition is coming from inner knowingness, logic is a mental and analytical process of figuring things out piece-by-piece, and emotion is following your feelings.)

2. Remember a time when you knew something through intuition.

3. Remember a time when you knew something through logic and reasoning. Tell me about it.

4. Remember a time when you knew something through your emotional feelings.

5. Repeat steps 2, 3, and 4 a few times.

It is most important to remember that first impressions are usually based on intuition. The next drill is an exercise in first impressions in order to train the client in intuition.

Exercise #2

Give the the following instructions to your client:

1. Give me your very first impression when you came into this room.

2. Describe this room analytically and logically.

3. Now describe the room to me from an emotional perspective.

4. Now choose a memorable person in your life and tell me your very first intuitive feeling about that person.

5. Describe that person to me in a logical way, using reasoning and deduction.

6. Describe that person to me in an emotional way—your emotional response to the person.

Repeat this exercise as many times and as often as you need to in order to perfect the client's understanding of the difference between intuition, logic and emotions.

DIFFERENCE BETWEEN INTUITION, LOGIC AND EMOTIONS

Intuition

1) Deep sense of knowing.

2) A person "just knows" but does not know how.

3) Comes in a flash, all-at-once understanding.

4) Often has a physical reaction associated with it.

Logic

1) Reasonable, analytical, linear (one thought follows another in logical sequence), intellectual.

2) Proves itself out through analysis and facts of tangible evidence.

3) Very mental and reasonable or rational.

4) Has to be figured out and pieced together bit-by-bit.

Emotions

1) Gut-level feeling.

2) Has feelings or emotional tone.

3) Emotions give the direction.

4) Feeling reaction in solar plexus; sticky, thick feeling.

STUDY QUESTIONS

1. List three ways of knowing.

2. What is the importance of intuition to the process of regression?

3. List the difference between knowledge through intuition, logic and emotions.

4. Have someone assist you through these exercises until you are thoroughly familiar with the difference between intuition and logic.

THOUGHTFORMS

Discuss with the client the notion that thoughts are made up of energy that contribute to creating reality. Thoughts have form just as material objects do. These thoughtforms will be used in regression work, so it is important to understand what they are.

A thoughtform actually has physical properties and influences your behavior. The thoughtform is the energy that one reacts to and can actually lead a person back to the past life where the thoughtform originated. For example, if a person has a pain or disease at the present time, the visual symbols in the thoughtform will be the same now (related to that pain or disease) as they were in the past life where the problem began. The present thoughtform originates in the past life experience. Example: If pain in the stomach feels like a heavy black piece of rock, there will have been a heavy black piece of rock in the past life that caused that pain.

Exercise #1

Give your client the following instructions:

1. Take an object, hold it in your hands and look at it carefully. Tell me what it is. Identify it for me.

   a. What color is it?

   b. What shape is it?

   c. What is its weight?

   d. What is its temperature?

   e. What is its substance?

   f. What is the texture?

   g. Where do you feel it on your body?

   h. What does it make you want to do?

   i. Does it keep you from doing anything?

   j. You have completed the thoughtform, so now erase it from your mind.

2. Recall a time when you had a really strong negative emotion. Identify the emotion.

   a. What color is it?

   b. What shape is it?

   c. What is its weight?

   d. What is its temperature?

   e. What is its substance?

   f. What is the texture?

   g. Where do you feel it on your body?

   h. What does it make you want to do?

   i. Does it keep you from doing anything?

   j. You have completed the thoughtform, so now erase it from your mind.

3. Recall a time when you had an illness or physical accident.

   a. What color is it?

   b. What shape is it?

   c. What is its weight?

   d. What is its temperature?

   e. What is its substance?

   f. What is the texture?

   g. Where do you feel it on your body?

   h. What does it make you want to do?

   i. Does it keep you from doing anything?

   j. You have completed the thoughtform, so now erase it from your mind.

Exercise #2

Continue by giving your client the following instructions:

1. I want you to think about a fixed belief you have about others such as, "People are not to be trusted." Be sure it is a very solid and rigid fixed belief—one that you strongly believe in.

2. Now tell me what the belief is. Identify it for me.

    a. What color is it?

    b. What shape is it?

    c. What is its weight?

    d. What is its temperature?

    e. What is its substance?

    f. What is the texture?

    g. Where do you feel it on your body?

    h. What does it make you want to do?

    i. Does it keep you from doing anything?

    j. You have completed the thoughtform, so now erase it from your mind.

Exercice #3

Give your client the following instructions:

1. Recall a time when something really nice happened to you.

2. Identify the feeling.

   a. What color is it?

   b. What shape is it?

   c. What is its weight?

   d. What is its temperature?

   e. What is its substance?

   f. What is the texture?

   g. Where do you feel it on your body?

   h. What does it make you want to do?

   i. Does it keep you from doing anything?

   j. You have completed the thoughtform, so now erase it from
       your mind.

IMPORTANT NOTE: These exercises and drills must be thoroughly done. It is important not to rush through them. As mentioned earlier, it is essential that the client be fully trained in each drill so the concept is clear and the experience is understood without any confusion or doubt. It is better to take plenty of time; perhaps devote the first session simply to doing the interview and drills if the person needs the time. The regression work can be done at subsequent sessions. The main thing is to fully prepare the client **before** the actual regression. The effectiveness of the regression depends on the thoroughness with which these preparation drills have been done. All of the skills gained in the drills will be used by the client in the course of doing past life regressions.

STUDY QUESTIONS

1. What is a thoughtform?

2. Which of these statements is right: "Thoughts create reality" or "Reality create thought?"

3. What is the importance of the thoughtforms to past life regression?

4. Have someone assist you through these exercises until the experience is understood.

IDENTIFICATION OF
THE LIFE LESSON

Identifying the lesson or major problem to be worked on is almost as important as the process itself. But first, a word of caution.

DragonPsychology does not advocate the use of past life regressions to handle various day-to-day issues that might be resolved through other techniques. The first preference is always to solve a problem or issue through techniques that work with the present. Why? The reasons are several. One is that we are attempting to teach people to live in the present rather than dwelling in the past. Another is that regression work can become very "glamorous" to people who want to find out all the dazzling dramatic stories of lives past. The emptier people's lives are in the present, the more they want to find a glamorous past. This could lead people to having regressions done for the wrong reasons, which would not serve the purpose of doing regressions.

The purpose of regression counseling is to resolve an issue or challenge that appears to reflect a major life lesson which does not have its cause or origin in this life. The way that you can determine whether it is a major life lesson is by answering the following:

1. Is it an issue that the client has made many attempts to handle through many different means including various therapies, without any success?

2. Is it a pattern in the client's life that has been repeated many times, especially in relationships?

3. Is it true that the origin of the problem cannot be found in this life? For example, having a strong fear of being raped, or a fear of birds, or a fear of heights, when there is no logical reason for that fear in this lifetime?

4. Are there strong physical symptoms associated with the issue or problem for which traditional doctors have not found a medical explanation? Some examples are having a sensation of being choked or being stabbed in the stomach, or a feeling of one's head being chopped off. In these cases, working in conjunction with a medical doctor is advised. <u>Regression counseling is one of the techniques of Dragon Psychology and is for the sole purpose of enhancing one's spiritual growth. Regression counseling does not in any way pretend to replace standard medical treatment.</u>

If any of the answers to the above questions is yes, then you have identified a major life lesson and a regression is appropriate.

In order to identify the life lesson, review the issue to find the symptoms the person is experiencing. Remember that the purpose is to identify the life lesson that the clients are working on. They will usually start out with a complaint or a problem that they are unable to solve. It is up to the counselor to take an inventory of all the information about the issue or problem and redefine it in terms of a life lesson. There are major and minor life lessons. A major life lesson is defined by the four criteria previously listed.

Here are some questions the counselor can use as guidelines to gather all pertinent information about the issue in order to identify the life lesson.

Ask the client:

1. What is the nature of the problem you are presently experiencing?

   a. How does it affect your relationships with others? Who are the primary players in this issue? To which of the players are you reacting the most?

   b. What are your emotional reactions? Name the primary emotions involved (fear, anger, hurt, sadness, loss, elation, depression, etc.).

   c. In this issue, of whom do you find yourself most critical?

   d. In your own words, what do you think is the major problem that you have been unable to solve?

   e. What is the issue that you do not want to confront? (NOTE: When you ask this question, you must be willing to wait for the answer. If the client starts to go blank, or starts to dance around the issue, then you know that you are getting closer.)

   f. What are the physical symptoms that you have been experiencing lately? Do you have any illnesses, tiredness, unusual complaints, or are there any areas of your body that have been going through changes?

          After a while, a pattern should start to develop. If this is a life lesson you should be able to combine everything that has come up into one whole. What you are doing is collecting all the pieces of a puzzle until they fit together into a whole picture.

When the life lesson is identified, the client should really be able to relate to and work with it. If the past life experience you contact during regression actually is the origin of the present life lesson, then all data and symptoms the clients gave in answer to the above questions should be present in the past life experience.

Clearly note the life lesson to be worked on during regression since you will be referring to it throughout the process.

STUDY QUESTIONS

1. What are the four criteria by which to determine if the problem your client is facing is a major life lesson?

2. What kind of questions would you ask in order to help your client identify a major life lesson?

3. Have someone help you identify one of your major life lessons which might be resolved by regression counseling.

STUDY QUESTIONS

1. Describe the exercise by which to determine if the problem you are working with is past-life related.

2. What kind of questions would you ask in order to help your client identify a possible problem?

3. How can your past-life experience help you understand life lessons which have not been fully resolved in this life?

MEDITATION STEPS
FOR REGRESSIONS

We would like to note here that a concise counselor's text for the meditation steps and the past life regression process itself has been outlined in Appendix A. The following is a run-through of both processes with an explanation for each step. It is very important that the counselor is familiar with the steps and the purpose for each before attempting to conduct a regression session.

In preparing someone for a regression, it is the counselor's responsibility to create an atmosphere of maximum receptiveness for the process to follow. For this reason, it is of utmost importance that the client be in a relaxed and responsive mood prior to the regression. The meditation and relaxation steps have been developed based on many years of research and practice by the authors. The meditation steps are intended to relax the clients by freeing them from all worries, tensions, and thoughts of everyday life so they can be fully awake, alert, and present for the regression.

<u>It should be noted here that hypnosis is not used because we believe that it fosters dependency.</u> In hypnosis, the counselor actually takes on the responsibility of resolving the client's problem. In Dragon Psychology, this means that the counselor is taking on or carrying someone else's karma or life lesson, and could begin to experience the same physical pains and problems as the client. This slows the progress of the counselor and interferes with the client's growth as well.

The meditation steps are outlined in this chapter in very simple terms, and we've stated the purpose for the more important steps. The counselor's task is to create the space for the client to achieve the intended purpose. The counselor cannot do the meditation for the client.

Before beginning the session, you as the counselor should visualize yourself surrounded by a crystal, light and love. It also is helpful to wear a crystal pendant around your neck over the heart area, because the crystal protects the counselor, and serves to transmit love energy from the heart.

While going through the steps of the meditation, send love and light to the client. During the rainbow meditation send each color to the client. The intention is to put the client in touch with his higher self or Guardian Angel. This also sets the stage to help the person see the life lesson in the context of the soul's evolution. That strong intention is the way to provide the most support to the client.

Preparation

1. Have the client choose whether to sit or lie down in a comfortable position. If he is sitting, make sure that it is with back straight and legs uncrossed. Let the client know that this position will have to be held for as long as one and a half hours. If the client is lying down, make sure there is a pillow. It is a good idea to have a blanket handy because many times the client will feel cold. Have lots of kleenex tissue available for emotional moments later in the regression.

2. Have the client clearly restate the life lesson to be handled in the regression. The lesson must be one that the client agrees to work on in the session.

Relaxation Steps

1. Say the following to the client,

"Now we are going to do a relaxation exercise. Close your eyes.
Stiffen and tighten your feet, then relax them. Now, stiffen your
legs and then relax them. Go through all of your body including
your legs, buttocks, stomach, chest, arms, neck, face, and
head. Tell me when you are completely and totally relaxed."
(Note: Let the client do this himself so he doesn't go into a
hypnotic trance. Be very careful not to put the client into a
trance.)

2. Then say,

"Take three deep breaths. Inhale to the count of seven, hold to
the count of seven, and exhale to the count of seven. Do this
three times, and as you inhale, visualize or experience energy
flowing through and around your body. Tell me how you
experience the energy or what kind of image you see." (Note:
the goal is to break up rigidity and encourage flexibility so the
client can change. This process also opens up the intuition.)

3. Say to the client,

"Visualize a white circle in front of you. Focus on any problems,
tensions, or worries that are on your mind other than those we
are working on today. Imagine pulling out these problems and
putting them into the white circle one by one. Tell me when you
are finished. (PAUSE) Now you can erase the white circle.
Check yourself again and tell me if there is anything else left on
your mind which might be troubling you." Repeat the process
until the client's mind is cleansed and purified and the circle is
erased and cleansed.

4. Tell the client,

"Now visualize yourself surrounded by a crystal and tell me its shape and size. (PAUSE) The crystal creates a safe place through which you can receive and transmit, yet it protects you. It is your own special safe place to be."

Purpose: Crystals have been used for ages to serve as protection for going between lives and dimensions. During regressions the client sometimes leaves his body, leaving it vulnerable to unhappy souls. This crystal meditation protects the client from this occurrence.

5. Say to the client,

"Go through your body and look for any areas of darkness or heaviness. Tell me what areas they are. (Note those areas down on paper.) Send those areas lots of love and light, until they are full of light and feel light in weight. See your whole body full of light."

Purpose: This is another process to clear any negativity. The dark areas will be the areas of the body that will have significance in the past life itself. Remember to make note of the dark areas.

At this point the client should be relaxed, allowing the person to go into a past life faster. From this point on, the counselor should use clear cut directions, and cut out any extraneous conversation or chit-chat.

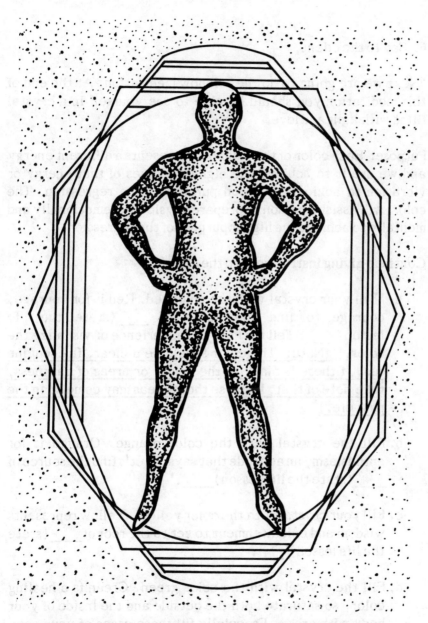

Crystals, the most highly-evolved member of the Mineral Kingdom, have traditionally served as protection for souls going between lives in the Human Kingdom.

6. Say to the client,

"Next we are going to do the rainbow meditation. At the end of this meditation you should be able to see yourself in a crystal filled with light and love.

Purpose: Each color of the rainbow represents a different energy and we use it to achieve the highest virtues of that energy or vibration to achieve the good purpose of the regression. The colors will assist a person to prepare physically, emotionally and mentally to achieve the higher purpose of the regression.

Continue giving instructions to the client:

   a. "Fill your crystal with the color red. Red is for courage, courage to find the cause of ____(state the life lesson)____. Tell me how you experience or visualize the color." (Note: The color should be a clear, fire-engine red. If there is black in the color, or areas of darkness, take note of that, because those areas may come up in the past life.)

   b. Fill the crystal with the color orange. Orange is for enthusiasm, an attitude that says, 'Let's find the source of ____(state the life lesson)____.'

   c. Fill your crystal with the color yellow. Yellow represents wisdom and enlightenment to get to the root of____(state the life lesson)____.

   d. Fill the crystal with the color green. Green is a healing color, so saturate both the outside and the inside of your body with green. Especially fill those areas of your body that you saw as dark with the color green.

e. Now saturate the crystal with the color blue. Blue stands for truth and integrity to resolve the issue of ____(state the life lesson)____.

f. Then saturate your crystal with purple. Purple stands for having the self-esteem to really handle the challenge of ____(state the life lesson)____.

g. Now saturate the crystal with violet, both inside your body as well as in the crystal. Violet is the most spiritual color, and the whole purpose in doing this regression is to aid your spiritual evolution.

h. All of these colors make up the full spectrum of pure white light. So now fill yourself and your crystal with a soft, glowing, white light. Look for any negativity or darkness in your body. If so, change it to love and send it back to where it came from, as we are working only with the light. When you are totally clear and filled with white light, we are ready to proceed."

You're now ready to take your client through the past life regression counseling process.

STUDY QUESTIONS

1. What might be a major disadvantage to using hypnosis in regression counseling?

2. What is the purpose for the meditation prior to regression?

3. What is the role of the crystal in regression counseling?

4. List the items you should have on hand before starting the regression process.

5. Outline the meditation steps.

The Steps
For Past Life
Regression Counseling

CONTENT

I. REGRESSION PROCESS

A summary of the past life regression process will provide a framework to help you understand the logic of each step.

The duty of the counselor is to assist clients in going back to a life time that contains the cause of a current-life problem. Once that life is contacted and recreated, the client must take responsibility for causing whatever happened and learn to see the life lesson in terms of his or her evolutionary growth. Then the energy is transmuted, the lesson learned and the script is rewritten to provide for a positive approach to the present and future.

The steps take the client from the most recent time of intensely experiencing the life lesson to the "karmic cause" lifetime - the past life that holds the key to the current life lesson. At this point the energy is transmuted, the underlying belief is changed and the client is brought back, step-by-step into the present where the script is rewritten.

A. THE MOST RECENT INTENSE EXPERIENCE OF THE LIFE LESSON

1. Say to the client,

"Tell me the most recent time you intensely experienced ____ (state the life lesson)____ . (Note: the key words are recent and intense.) I want you to be there to re-experience it and tell me what is going on."

2. At this point the person will describe to you the situation. Often this will be a very recent event still fresh in his mind accompanied by strong emotions and physical sensations. If the client is having some difficulty orienting himself in the memory recall, you can assist him to re-experience the situation by asking the following questions:

    a.   What time of the year is it?

    b. Where are you (inside/outside)?

    c. Describe what's around you.

    d. Are you standing up, sitting, or lying down?

    e. Who else is there with you?

    f. What's the action? What's going on?

    g. Describe your physical reactions.

h. Describe your emotional reactions.

i. Describe your mental reactions.

3. After the client has fully described the situation and his reactions to it physically, emotionally and mentally, ask,

"In your mind, how were you the cause of the situation?"

(Note: It is very important that the client takes responsibility and not get stuck in feeling like a victim.)

4. Then ask,

"Is there anything more you would like to say about this situation?"

Go to the next step after the client finishes.

B.   THE THOUGHTFORM OF THIS RECENT EXPERIENCE

Remember that the thoughtform is the energy that creates reality. So the next step is to find the thoughtform of this most recent event. The thoughtform is the energy that will take the client back to the karmic cause lifetime.

1. Explain to the client,

"Now we want to identify the thoughtform of what you've just experienced, so stay with your feelings and thoughts, and answer the following questions by saying the first thing that comes to your mind."

Then ask the client (recording the answers):

   a.   What color is it?

   b.   What size is it?

   c.   What shape is it?

   d. What is its weight? (Have him describe in concrete terms such as comparisons or actual weight. If he says heavy, then ask, 'How heavy (a ton/100 pounds)?')

   e.   What is its temperature?

   f.   What is its substance?

   g.   What is its texture?

h. Where do you feel it on your body? (You can show me with your hand.)

i. What does it make you want to do?

j. Does it keep you from doing anything?

2. The counselor must record all this data because he will use it later to verify the karmic cause lifetime. If you have actually gone to the karmic cause lifetime of the life lesson, the lifetime where this life lesson originated, then all the characteristics listed here will be present in the original lifetime.

C. MOST–INTENSE EXPERIENCE OF THE LESSON IN THIS LIFETIME

1. Say to your client,

"Now let us go back in time to the most intense, most memorable time in this lifetime where you experienced_____(state life lesson)_____. Allow yourself to be there, and tell me what is going on."

2. Help in recalling details:

The client may need some time to get to that place, or he may immediately start telling you the situation. Watch his reactions and let him be the guide. Since we are relying on memory that may have previously been blocked from his conscious mind, you may need to assist the client to be there again. You can do that by encouraging the use of the senses.

Ask the following questions:

    a.   What do you smell?

    b.   Do you hear anything?

    c.   Feel around you. What do you feel?

    d.   Look at your hands. How old are you?

    e.   Look down at your clothes. What are you wearing?

    f. What time of the year is it?

    g. Where are you (inside/outside)?

    h. Describe what's around you.

    i. Are you standing up, sitting, or lying down?

    j. What's the action? What's going on?

    k. Who else is there with you?

    l. What are your physical reactions?

    m. What are your emotional reactions?

    n. What are your mental reactions?"

3. Helping client deal with strong emotions:

With your guidance, the person should now be telling you exactly what is going on and his reactions to the situation. If this is a life lesson that is mainly physical, then you can expect the client to have lots of physical symptoms and reactions. If the lesson is more emotional, then the client will probably express strong emotions. If it is more a mental life lesson, then you will find more of a emotionally detached description, but the client may try to avoid the emotions by blanking out, sidestepping your questions, or simply not answering the questions.

For clients working on an emotional life lesson, you should have lots of tissue available, and make it safe for them to express those emotions. The emotional release is actually very healing for the client so do not try to stop it.

If, however, the emotional and/or physical reactions are actually keeping the client from looking at the situation or causing undue pain, then the counselor can assist the person to detach by saying,

"Now go back to a time before this all happened which is safe. I want you to go above the situation and be the observer. You don't have to re-experience the pain. View the situation as if you are watching a movie. Now, tell me what is happening as if you are describing a movie." (Note: Remember to use this technique for any intense emotional reaction during the rest of the regression process.

4.   When the client comes to the actual time of trauma or emotional reaction, ask,

"What decision did you make at this time?"

Note: This is where strong beliefs are actually born; where a person decides, "It doesn't pay to   ," or "I'm never going to   ." These beliefs are very important to note and to work with in the transmuting process that comes later.)

5. Claiming accountability for the experience:

After the person has completed describing the situation, you can assist him to see how he was the cause of what happened. This is a very important step, because if the person stays in the victim frame of mind, she is likely to lead you to a lifetime where she was a victim instead of the karmic cause lifetime, or the lifetime of the original experience. So ask the client,

"How were you the cause of this situation? On which lesson were you working?"

6. Finally, ask,

"Are you finished? Is there anything more you want to say?"

D. EARLIEST EXPERIENCE OF THE LIFE LESSON IN THIS LIFETIME

1. Tell your client, "Using your intuition, I'd like you to go back in time to the first time in this life that you experienced _____ (state life lesson) _____ ."

Then ask the following questions:

    a. "What do you smell?

    b. Do you hear anything?

    c. Feel around you. What do you feel?

    d. Look at your hands. How old are you?

    e. Look down at your clothes. What are you wearing?

    f. What time of year is it?

    g. Where are you (inside/outside)?

    h. Describe what's around you.

    i. Are you standing up, sitting, or lying down?

    j. What's the action? What's going on?

    k. Who else is there with you?

    l. What are your physical reactions?

m. What are your emotional reactions?

n. What are your mental reactions?

2. When the person comes to the major reaction, ask,

"What decision did you make at this time?"

3. Assist the client in being accountable by asking,

"In your mind, how were you the cause of this situation? On what lesson were you working?"

4. Finally, make sure that everything was covered by saying,

"Are you finished? Is there anything more you want to add?"

Continue after you are sure that the client has completed.

E. EXPERIENCE AT THE TIME OF BIRTH

1. Say to your client,

"Now move to the time of your birth — to the actual time of delivery. See if_____(state life lesson)_____was there at that time. Put yourself back to the actual time of birth, and tell me:

    a. What do you smell?

    b. Do you hear anything?

    c. Feel around you. What do you feel?

    d. What emotions are you experiencing?

    e. What thoughts are you having?

    f. Describe what's around you.

    g. What's going on?

    h. Who else is there with you? How are you feeling towards that person?

    i. What decision did you make at this time?

    j. Is____(state life lesson)____with you now?

    k. How were you the cause of this situation? What is the
       lesson you are trying to learn?"

NOTE: If the client can't intuitively tell what is happening at birth in this present lifetime, then he will not be able to go to a past lifetime either. This step is a good barometer as to whether or not the client is prepared for past life regression.

If he cannot do the birth section, go back and do the intuition drill because he has to master it in order to be regressed.

The client may experience an intense emotional release while reliving his or her birth, and sometimes the actual cause can be located here. If all the symptoms of the thoughtform are here, then this is actually the cause, and you need not proceed to the past life portion. Instead, you should double check the thoughtform, go to the transmutation process and then rescript each step of the regression to the present. At that point you are finished with the process.

If the client has been taking a victim position in all of the events so far and has not been able to see that he is at cause, then he will probably only regress to a victim lifetime rather than the cause lifetime. In this case we recommended that you stop the process after the birth cycle. You will need to do the victim, blame and accountability processes with this client before he is ready for another regression. He will probably not be very successful rewriting the script of his life lesson at each step of the regression process because he sees himself as a victim. Therefore the counselor need not go through those steps.

If, however, the client had good recall of his birth but did not get release or did not discover the cause, then continue to the next step.

F. EXPERIENCE OF THE LIFE LESSON DURING KARMIC CAUSE LIFETIME

1. Say to the client,

"Now I want you to follow your intuition and go to the karmic cause lifetime. This is where it all started, where you were actually the cause. So be there, re-experience it, and tell me what is going on." (Note: Give the client time to get to that place and tell you what he perceives. It may be vague at first. Help the client get oriented by encouraging her to use her senses.)

Say, "I want you to open up your senses and tell me:

    a. What do you smell?

    b. What do you hear?

    c. What is the most distinct taste (even if it is in the air)?

    d. What time of year is it?

    e. What time of day or night is it?

    f. Look at your hands. Are they the hands of a man or a woman? How old are you?"

2. Continue by saying,

"Move into your body or form and look out of your eyes and tell me what you perceive. What I want you to do now is to focus in on the situation in that life where_____(state the life lesson)_____began in the first place. What was the situation?

 a. Describe what is around you.

 b. Tell me intuitively, what country you are in.

 c. What time period is it?

 d. What is the action? What is going on?"

3. Helping clients give themselves permission for personal accountability:

It is often very difficult for people to face how they actually created the situation they are in. In the karmic cause lifetime we created the cause of our problem by taking some strong action, often negative, that left us with a strong impression on the basis of which we made certain decisions. This belief or decision has actually been lived out in many lifetimes to follow. The confrontation is mostly about protecting that "good guy" image that everyone would like to preserve. If you feel the client is resisting looking at how he was the cause, you can assist him in breaking through this barrier by helping him create the permission he needs in order to look at his negative actions.

Say to the client,

"How will looking at how you are the cause in this situation help you? Can you give yourself permission to see what actions you took in that lifetime without judging or blaming yourself so that you can really solve this issue?" (Note: Let the client tell you in his own words about the situation.)

Then ask,

"In your mind, what caused this situation or brought it about in the first place?"

The response may show that the client is taking some responsibility for the situation. Gear your questions to guide the person to see, acknowledge, and own his actions that were the cause in this lifetime. Use your intuition to guide him.

If the client continues to be a victim, ask,

"Go back a little before this situation. What was it that caused you to get into this predicament?"

Your purpose is to find out how the client brought about the karmic cause through his actions in that lifetime. If it becomes clear that the client does not want to look at that, then drop the subject. Know that you will have to do a lot of counseling with this person to help him see how he is at cause. Some people are simply not ready to look at their own responsibility. With someone like this who finds security in being a victim, he needs the space to talk for several sessions about his pain and suffering before he is ready to let go of being victim. For him being heard is most important. Use your judgment with a person like this.

4. When you get to the actions that were the cause, ask,

"What decision did you make at this time? Are there any other decisions that you made as a result of this situation?" (Note: What you are looking for is the basic belief that underlies the life lesson).

5. Key players in that lifetime are more than likely present in this lifetime, so if part of the purpose is to identify the client's connection to someone, then you say,

"Look deep into the eyes of ____(the player)____ and tell me, who is that person in your present life? Use your intuition and tell me the first person that comes to mind."

6. Then, find out what the consequences of the actions were in that lifetime. Ask,

"What were the results of your actions in that lifetime? Where did you end up? How did you live out that lifetime? How did you die?"

7. To make sure that the client has completed, ask,

"Is there anything more you want to say? Are you finished?"

8. Now, refer to your notes and check out the details on the original thoughtform which you recorded at the beginning of the regression process. Read back the properties one by one, asking,

"Tell me where you find the color ____(say color)____ in this lifetime. Is there something____(say shape)___ around?"

Continue until you have covered and identified all the qualities in the thoughtform. This is how the thoughtform reappears in the past life. For example, a person described the thoughtform as cone-shaped, large, and red, and felt it in his chest. When he got to the past life where this emotion began, he found a cone-shaped, red object stabbing him to death in the chest. He took a mental picture of that object, and it has haunted him ever since. That thoughtform took on a life of its own because it was a lesson that needed to be completed. Every time a similar experience comes up (in order to finish that lesson) in lifetimes to follow, that thoughtform or image will be brought back to life.

The thoughtform serves as a confirmation that this is the correct karmic cause lifetime in which the life lesson originated.

II. TRANSMUTATION PROCESS

The regression process has now been completed, and we can proceed to rewrite the script and complete the unfinished lesson. The aim is to change our underlying belief as we retrace the life lesson through the regression steps to the present time.

A. KARMIC CAUSE LIFETIME WHEN LIFE LESSON ORIGINATED

1. The first step is to examine the unfinished lesson. Ask:

"What is the unfinished lesson you have been carrying since that time?" Wait for the response.

Then ask:

"Are you willing to complete this lesson of ____ (state the life lesson)____ right now?"

2. The next step is to turn the negativity into positivity by saying to the client:

"In every situation, there is a positive and a negative. Look at that situation and tell me what you learned that was positive. How has that become one of your attributes now?"

Then ask,

"Knowing what you know today, if you could rewrite that script, how would you rewrite it? Instead of _____ (say life lesson)_____, with what would you replace it? How could you change that energy or situation so everyone can win? Instead of ____ (name life lesson)____, what would the new experience be called?"

The purpose here is to assist clients to rewrite the past according to where they are currently on their evolution in a positive manner that allows everyone to win. The actual form that the changes take is not so important because there are many ways to achieve a positive end. Each client must do it in a way that works best for him or her. At each step, the client will be asked to now see the old life lesson in terms of the changes he has made in his belief.

It is important that each situation which has been recalled in this whole regression procedure be changed to positive energy.

B. EXPERIENCE AT THE TIME OF BIRTH

Say to the client,

"Now return to birth and tell me how it would have been with your birth with this new experience. Now recreate it with the new vibration."

C. EARLIEST EXPERIENCE OF THE LIFE LESSON IN THIS LIFETIME

Continue to transmute the old life lesson by saying to the client,

"Return to the first time in this lifetime that you experienced the old emotion and write a new, positive script. Tell me how it would have been if you did not have ____(name the old life lesson)____, but instead had ____(name the new experience)."

D. MOST INTENSE EXPERIENCE OF THE LIFE LESSON IN THIS LIFETIME

Then say to the client,

"Now look at the time in this lifetime that you most intensely experienced ____(name old life lesson)____. Now rewrite the script using the new energy or emotions of ___(name new experience) and see how it would have been different."

E. MOST RECENT EXPERIENCE OF THE LIFE LESSON IN THIS LIFETIME

To help the client continue to rewrite the script, say,

"Finally, look at the most recent time you experienced ____(name old life lesson)___. Rewrite the script using the new energy or emotions of____(name new experience)___ and tell me how it would have been different."

F. FUTURE

To complete the process, say to the client,

"Now look to see if there is any last piece of the old experience of
___(name old life lesson)___in your mind, body, or emotions. In
your mind, thank the energy of ___(name old life lesson)___ for
being present in your life with its good purpose, and affirm that
you have now learned the lesson it was helping you to learn.
(PAUSE) Send this old energy on its way now, because it has now
completed its work. (PAUSE) Go through your body, starting
with your head and going all the way through your body to your
feet and see that energy leaving. Pay special attention to those
areas that were most affected by the energy. Now go through
your body and replace it with the new energy of ___(name the
new experience)___. Fill every cell in your body with the new
energy. (PAUSE) Remember that your thoughts create your
reality. Now let's look at the new thoughtform that goes with the
new experience.

    a. What color is it?

    b. What size is it?

    c. What shape is it?

    d. What is its weight?

    e. What is its temperature?

    f. What is it made up of?

g. What is its sound?

h. What is the texture?

i. Where do you feel it on your body?

j. What does it make you want to do?

k. Does it keep you from doing anything?

l. How would you walk with your new vibration? Talk? Dress?

Then say,

> "See yourself very clearly with this new energy and come back into the room. Become aware of the surroundings in this room. Now open your eyes. Focus on an object in this room and tell me something beautiful about it. Find something else in the room and tell me something good about it."

The regression process is now complete. You have assisted the client in going back to the cause of his life lesson, to see how he was responsible for creating his own effects which he has been living out until now. You have helped him re-evaluate his life lesson from the larger framework of his overall evolutionary progress. Finally, you have helped him to transmute the energy, or complete the unfinished lesson by rewriting the past into a new, more positive and up-to-date vibration more in line with his present state of evolution. This means that you have helped the client recreate the past, so he can turn his attention to the present and become cause in the here-and-now. In this way, the person can create more and more positive effects for the future.

SUMMARY OF THE
CLIENT'S REGRESSION
EXPERIENCE

At the end of the counseling session, it is important that clients summarize their past life regression experiences and the value they derived from the process. Please ask each client to write a brief summary in this format:

1. Write a brief summary of the past life experience no longer than one page.

2. Describe your reactions, a) physically, b) emotionally and c) mentally.

3. What was the decision that you made at that time? How has that decision affected this life?

4. What was your reason for doing a past life regression?

5. Fill in the form with your name and address, your counselor's name and date. (See the form at the end of the "Counselor's Text.")

SUMMARY OF CLIENT'S REGRESSION EXPERIENCE

CLIENT'S
NAME_____

ADDRESS_____

COUNSELOR'S
NAME_____

DATE OF
SESSION_____

To the client:

It is important to summarize your regression experience and the
value that you've derived from it. For this reason, we suggest
you write a brief summary in the following format:

1. Write a brief summary of the past life experience no longer
   than one page.

2. Describe your reactions, a) physically, b) emotionally and
   c) mentally.

3. What was the decision that you made at that time? How has
   that decision affected this life?

4. What was your reason for doing a past life regression?

_____

STUDY QUESTIONS

1. Outline the sequence for the regression process.

2. What is the meaning of "karmic cause" lifetime?

3. What are some of the questions you can ask your clients to help them relive the experience of a life lesson?

   Recent intense experience:

   Thoughtform:

   Most intense experience in this lifetime:

The earliest experience:

Experience at the time of birth:

Karmic cause lifetime experience:

4. How can you assist a person detach from a strong emotional and/or physical reaction to a past life?

5. Why is it very important to assist your clients in accepting accountability for whatever has happened in past lives?

6. What should you do if your client can't intuitively describe the birth scene?

7. What should you do if a client has a intense emotional release while reliving the birth scene?

8. How can you best help clients who get stuck in a lifetime where they see themselves as victims?

9. How can you help your clients give themselves permission to become accountable for the decisions that created their life lessons?

10. What is the purpose of the transmutation process?

APPENDIX A

Following is a counselor's text for doing past life regression counseling. This is a straight text, uninterrupted by explanations. Please be certain that you understand the entire process thoroughly before using this regression text.

COUNSELOR'S TEXT
FOR DOING REGRESSIONS*

I. MEDITATION STEPS FOR REGRESSION

Have your client get comfortable. Provide a blanket and pillow and have facial tissue on hand. You will need pen and paper to record the client's answers, when necessary.

Give your client the following instructions:

1. State the life lesson you have chosen to work on.

---

*This text is purposely written in an informal language to assist the counselor to create a relaxed atmosphere for the client.

2. Now we are going to do a relaxation exercise. Close your eyes. Stiffen and tighten your feet, then relax them. Now, stiffen your legs and then relax them. Go through all of your body including your legs, buttocks, stomach, chest, arms, neck, face and head, stiffening and relaxing each part. Tell me when you are completely and totally relaxed.

3. Take three deep breaths. Inhale to the count of seven, hold to the count of seven, and exhale to the count of seven. Do this three times, and as you inhale, visualize or experience energy flowing through and around your body. Tell me how you experience the energy or what kind of image you see.

4. Visualize a white circle in front of you. Focus on any problems, tensions, or worries that are on your mind other than those we are working on today. Imagine pulling out these problems and putting them into the white circle one by one. Tell me when you are finished. (PAUSE) Now you can erase the white circle. Check yourself again and tell me if there is anything else left on your mind which might be troubling you. (Note: repeat the process until the client has erased all problems.)

5. Now visualize yourself surrounded by a crystal and tell me its shape and size. (PAUSE) The crystal creates a safe place through which you can receive and transmit, yet is protection for you. It is your own special, safe place to be.

6. Go through your body and look for any areas of darkness or heaviness. Tell me what areas they are. (Note those areas down on paper.) Send those areas lots of love and light, until they are full of light and feel light in weight. See your whole body full of light.

7. Next we are going to do the rainbow meditation. At the end of this meditation you should be able to imagine yourself in a crystal filled with light and love.

   a. Fill your crystal with the color red. Red is for courage-- courage to find the cause of ____(state the life lesson)____. Tell me how you experience (visualize) the color. (Note: The color should be a clear, fire-engine red. If there is black in the color, or areas of darkness, take note of that, because those areas may come up in the past life.)

   b. Fill the crystal with the color orange. Orange is for enthusiasm -- an attitude that says, 'Let's find the source of____(state the life lesson)____.'

   c. Fill your crystal with the color yellow. Yellow represents wisdom and enlightenment to get to the root of____(state the life lesson)____.

   d. Fill the crystal with the color green. Green is a healing color, so saturate both the outside and the inside of your body with green. Especially fill those areas of your body that you saw as dark with the color green.

   e. Now saturate the crystal with the color blue. Blue stands for truth and integrity to resolve the issue of____(state the life lesson)____.

   f. Then saturate your crystal with purple. Purple stands for having the self-esteem to really handle the challenge of ____(state the life lesson)____.

g. Now saturate the crystal with violet, both inside your body as well as in the crystal. Violet is the most spiritual color, and the whole purpose in doing this regression is to aid your spiritual evolution.

h. All of these colors make up the full spectrum of pure white light. So now fill yourself and your crystal with a soft, glowing, white light. Look for any negativity or darkness in your body. If so, change it to love and send it back to where it came from, as we are working only with the light. When you are totally clear and filled with white light, we are ready to proceed."

II. PAST LIFE REGRESSION PROCESS

A. MOST RECENT INTENSE EXPERIENCE OF LIFE LESSON

Ask your client the following questions:

1. Tell me the most recent time you intensely experienced ____(state the life lesson)____. I want you to be there to re-experience it and tell me what is going on.

   a. What time of the year is it?
   b. Where are you (inside/outside)?
   c. Describe what is around you.
   d. Are you standing up, sitting, or lying down?
   e. Who else is there with you?
   f. What's the action? What is going on?
   g. Describe your physical reactions.
   h. Describe your emotional reactions.
   i. Describe your mental reactions.

2. In your mind, how were you the cause of the situation? How did you set up the situation?

3. Is there anything more you would like to say about this situation?

B. THOUGHTFORM

1. Now we want to identify the thoughtform of what you just experienced, so stay with your feelings and thoughts, and answer the questions by saying the first thing that comes to your mind.

   a. What color is it?
   b. What size is it?
   c. What shape is it?
   d. What is its weight? (Have him describe in concrete terms such as comparisons or actual weight. If he says heavy, then ask, 'How heavy (a ton/100 pounds)?')
   e. What is its temperature?
   f. What is its sound?
   g. What is its substance?
   h. What is the texture?
   i. Where do you feel it on your body? (You can show me with your hand.)
   j. What does it make you want to do?
   k. Does it keep you from doing anything?

(Note: The counselor needs to record all this data to be used later to verify the karmic cause lifetime or the lifetime where the life lesson originated.)

C. MOST INTENSE EXPERIENCE OF THE LIFE LESSON IN THIS LIFETIME

Give the following instructions to the client:

1. Now let's go back to the most intense, most memorable time this lifetime when you experienced _____(state life lesson)____. Allow yourself to be there, and tell me what is going on.

   a. What do you smell?
   b. Do you hear anything?
   c. Feel around you. What do you feel?
   d. Now, look at your hands. How old are you?
   e. Look down at your clothes. What are you wearing?
   f. What time of year is it?
   g. Where are you (inside/outside)?
   h. Describe what is around you.
   i. Are you standing up, sitting, or lying down?
   j. What is the action? What is going on?
   k. Who else is there with you?
   l. What are your physical reactions?
   m. What are your emotional reactions?
   n. What are your mental reactions?

2. (Optional -- use only if necessary to help clients deal with strong emotional reactions.)

Now go back to a time before this all happened which is safe. I want you to rise above the situation and be the observer. You do not have to re-experience the pain. View the situation as if you are watching a movie. Now, tell me what is happening as if you are describing a movie. (Remember to use this technique any time an event brings up a strong emotion during the rest of the regression.)

3. What decision did you make at this time?

4. How are you the cause of this situation? On which lesson were you working?

5. Are you finished? Is there anything more you want to say?

D. EARLIEST EXPERIENCE OF THE LIFE LESSON
IN THIS LIFETIME

Give the client the following instructions:

1. Using your intuition, I would like you to go back in time to the first time in this life that you experienced ____(state life lesson)____.

    a. What do you smell?
    b. Do you hear anything?
    c. Feel around you. What do you feel?
    d. Now, look at your hands. How old are you?
    e. Look down at your clothes. What are you wearing?
    f. What time of year is it?
    g. Where are you (inside/outside)?
    h. Describe what's around you.
    i. Are you standing up, sitting, or lying down?
    j. What is the action? What is going on?
    k. Who else is there with you?
    l. What are your physical reactions?
    m. What are your emotional reactions?
    n. What are your mental reactions?

2. What decision did you make at this time?

3. In your mind, how were you the cause of this situation? On which lesson were you working?

4. Are you finished? Is there anything more you want to add?

E. EXPERIENCE AT THE TIME OF BIRTH

Give the client the following instructions:

1. Now move to the time of your birth — to the actual time of delivery. See if____(state life lesson)____was there at that time. Put yourself back to the actual time of birth, and tell me:

    a. What do you smell?
    b. Do you hear anything?
    c. Feel around you. What do you feel?
    d. What emotions are you experiencing?
    e. What thoughts are you having?
    f. Describe what is around you.
    g. What is going on?
    h. Who else is there with you? How are you feeling towards that person?
    i. What decision did you make at this time?
    j. Is____(state life lesson)____with you now?
    k. How were you the cause of this situation? What is the lesson you are trying to learn?

F. EXPERIENCE OF THE LIFE LESSON DURING KARMIC CAUSE LIFETIME

1. Now I want you to follow your intuition and go to the karmic cause lifetime. This is where it all started, where you were actually the cause. So be there, re-experience it, and tell me what is going on. (Give the client time to get to that place and tell you what is perceived. It may be vague at first.)

Open up your senses and tell me:

   a. What do you smell?
   b. What do you hear?
   c. What is the most distinct taste (even if it is in the air)?
   d. What time of year is it?
   e. What time of day or night is it?
   f. What is the most distinct taste (even if it's in the air)?
   g. Look at your hands. Are they the hands of a man or a woman? How old are you?

2. Move into your body or form and look out of your eyes and tell me what you perceive. What I want you to do now is to focus in on the situation in that life where _____ (state the life lesson)_____ began in the first place. What was the situation?

   a. Describe what is around you.
   b. Tell me intuitively, what country you are in.
   c. What time period is it?
   d. What is the action? What is going on?

3. How will looking at how you are cause in this situation help you? Can you give yourself permission to see what actions

you took in that lifetime without judging or blaming yourself so that you can really solve this issue? In your mind, what caused this situation or brought it about in the first place?

Optional--use if the client sees herself as a victim.) Let's go back a little before this situation. What was it that caused you to get into that situation?

4. (When you get to the actions that were the cause ask,) What decision did you make at this time? Are there any other decisions that you made as a result of this situation? Remember that what you are looking for is the basic belief that underlies the life lesson.)

5. Look deep into the eyes of ____(the player)____ and tell me, who is that person in your present life? Use your intuition and tell me the first person that comes to mind.

6. What were the results of your actions in that lifetime? Where did you end up? How did you live out that lifetime? How did you die?

7. Is there anything more you want to say? Are you finished?

8. (Note: Refer to your notes and check out the details on the original thoughtform recorded at the beginning of the regression process. Read back the properties one by one. Say,)

    Tell me where you find the color_____(say color)_____in this lifetime. Is there something_____(say shape)_____around? (Continue until you have covered and identified all the qualities in their thoughtform. This is how the thoughtform reappears in the past life.)

III. TRANSMUTATION PROCESS

(The regression process has now been completed, and we can proceed to rewrite the script and complete the unfinished lesson.)

A. KARMIC CAUSE LIFETIME WHEN LIFE LESSON ORIGINATED

1. What is the unfinished lesson you have been carrying around since that lifetime where the problem originated? Are you willing to complete this lesson of ____(state the life lesson)____right now?

2. In every situation, there is a positive and a negative. Look at what you learned from that situation that was positive. What did you learn from that situation? How has that become one of your attributes now?

3. Knowing what you know today, if you could rewrite that script, how would you rewrite it? Instead of ____(say life lesson)____, with what would you replace it? How could you change it so that everyone can win? What would you name the new experience instead of____(name life lesson)____?

B. EXPERIENCE AT THE TIME OF BIRTH

Now return to birth and tell me how it would have been with your birth with this new experience. Recreate it now with the new energy.

C. EARLIEST EXPERIENCE OF THE LIFE LESSON IN THIS LIFETIME

Now return to the first time in this lifetime that you experienced the old emotion, and write a new, positive script. Tell me how it would have been if you did not have ____(name the old life lesson)____, but instead had____(name the new experience)?

D. MOST INTENSE EXPERIENCE OF THE LIFE LESSON IN THIS LIFETIME

Now look at the time this lifetime that you most intensely experienced____(name old life lesson)____. Rewrite the script using the new energy of____(name new experience)____and see how it would have been different.

E. MOST RECENT EXPERIENCE OF THE LIFE LESSON IN THIS LIFETIME

Finally, look at the most recent time you experienced ____(name old life lesson)____. Rewrite the script using the new energy of ____(name new experience)____and tell me how it would have been different.

F. FUTURE EXPERIENCE

1. Now look to see if there is any last piece of this old____(name life lesson)____ in your mind, body, or emotions. In your mind, thank the energy of ____(name life lesson)____ for being present in your life with its good purpose, and affirm that you have now learned the lesson it was helping you to learn. Send the old life lesson on its way now, because it has now completed its work.

   Go through your body, starting with your head and going all the way through your body to your feet and see that energy leaving. Pay special attention to those areas of the body that were most affected by the energy. Now go through your body and replace it with the new energy of ____(name the new experience)____. Fill every cell in your body with the new energy. Now let us do a new thoughtform--the new belief that will support this new experience.

   a. What color is it?
   b. What size is it?
   c. What shape is it?
   d. What is its weight?
   e. What is its temperature?
   f. What is it made up of?
   g. What is its sound?
   h. What is the texture?
   i. Where do you feel it on your body?
   j. What does it make you want to do?
   k. Does it keep you from doing anything?
   l. How would you walk with your new vibration? Talk? Dress?

2. See yourself very clearly with this new vibration and come
   back into the room. Become aware of the surroundings in this
   room. Now open your eyes. Focus on an object in this room
   and tell me something beautiful about it. Find something else
   in the room and tell me something good about it.

APPENDIX B

OUTLINE FOR REGRESSIONS

I. MEDITATION STEPS

1. Lie or sit down

2. State the life lesson to be worked on

3. Relax the body (tighten and release exercise)

4. Three deep breaths

5. White circle

6. Crystal

7. Darkness to light

8. Rainbow Meditation

    a. Red - courage

    b. Orange - enthusiasm

    c. Yellow - wisdom, enlightenment, knowledge

    d. Green - healing, inside and outside the body

e. Blue - honesty and integrity

f. Purple - self-esteem

g. Violet - spiritual, inside and outside body

h. Soft, white light

II. REGRESSION PROCESS

1. Most Recent Intense Experience of the Life Lesson

2. Thoughtform

3. Most Intense Experience of Life Lesson in This Lifetime

4. Earliest Experience of Life Lesson in This Lifetime

5. Experience at Time of Birth

6. Karmic Cause Lifetime When Life Lesson Originated

III. TRANSMUTATION PROCESS

1. Karmic Cause Lifetime When Life Lesson Originated

2. Experience at Time of Birth

3. Earliest Experience of Life Lesson in This Lifetime

4. Most Intense Experience of Life Lesson in This Lifetime

5. Most Recent Intense Experience of Life Lesson

6. Future (Thoughtform)

The real goal of life's journey is to break the birth-death cycle and evolve into the Immortal Kingdom.

Part III
Personal Experiences
of The Regression Process
Is It Memory Or Is It
Imagination?

This section provides answers to questions about the validity of reincarnation and past life regression.

What follows are a series of interviews with clients as well as personal testimonies. These are meant to answer a variety of questions about the regression process itself, the different types of people who have been regressed, age of clients, regression and illnesses, etc. Each is a lesson in past life regression counseling.

Except for minor editing for clarity, the interviews and testimonies are in the words of the clients. We have left analysis of the experience up to the reader.

ARE WE BORN
INTO DIFFERENT RACES?

Bob Sperling is a very handsome young Caucasian man in his late twenties or early thirties. He was courageous enough to share his identity and his interview about past lives, a subject that is still highly controversial. We appreciate his contribution to this book.

Bob's case was chosen to show that people are members of other races in former existences. Bob was a negro tribesman in Africa in one life. In another life, he was a young Egyptian girl. The experience of past lives as members of other races is quite common. It is almost always accompanied by a realization of the equality of the races and the unity of mankind, along with a desire to end the separation that currently exists among people throughout the world. Through this knowledge of past lives, racists will be surprised to find that in a former existence they were members of the very races they are warring against now.

Interview #1

Q - Tell me your name and where you live.

A - Bob Sperling, and I live presently in Winnetka, California.

Q - What is your occupation?

A - I work in the tax assessor's office, although I am planning to change vocations shortly.

Q - Why did you decide to have a past life regression?

A - I felt I had emotional blockages in my life that were keeping me from realizing certain ambitions and desires I had. Also, I had been led to believe that past life regression could help me deal with these blockages, which I now know is true.

Q - Can you describe yourself in a past life?

A - Yes. I was male and lived in the jungle in Africa. I was black and about thirty-three.

Q - Do you know your name in that life?

A - No.

Q - Can you say what time period it was?

A - It seemed like about the mid-eighteen hundreds.

Q - What was the situation in that past life?

A - I was a native tribesman and a healer for my tribe. I had attempted to heal a young boy but was unsuccessful. He died, despite my efforts. The members of the tribe rejected me, and I was forced to leave the village. I felt the rejection enormously, so I went into the jungle with the intention of finding a pit built to catch lions. When I found the pit there was a female lioness at the bottom prowling restlessly. She was beneath the spears that had been set up to impale any lion that might fall into the pit. The spears radiated from the sides of the pit towards the center, about two thirds of the way down, as if to form a wheel. I immediately felt a oneness with the lion; I felt she knew I had come there to kill myself. I jumped into the pit sort of like you would jump into a swimming pool to do a bomber dive; I jumped up into the air and my feet fell first into the pit. I felt myself falling down through and breaking the spears, then my spirit left my body as the lioness clawed me to death.

Q - What senses were you aware of? Could you hear, feel, smell or see?

A - Mainly I was aware of the sense of sight. I didn't really attempt to see if I could smell. I was aware of touch, because I could feel the spears as I fell through them. Basically, I observed the whole thing and was a little more detached than I would be if I were regressed back now. It was my first time being regressed, and I was a little aloof. If I went back now, I would try to experience it totally.

Q - What emotions were you aware of in that life?

A - I felt very hurt when I was rejected by the tribe. I felt that they didn't understand me and, in fact, no one could understand me. It may seem strange but, when I reached the pit, the emotion was a feeling of joy of being at oneness with the lioness. Also, I felt relief as I jumped and fell into the pit.

Q - How do you think the knowledge of this past life will help you now and in the future?

A - I now understand the feeling of rejection I've had all this life and now see why I've felt no one could understand me. I know also, why I've had a fear of sharp objects, falling, and also of heights. As for fear of rejection, I no longer will be operating within a framework of acceptance and rejection when dealing with people. I accept myself for what I am and other people for what they are. Basically, I have always accepted others and liked them. The problem was in not liking myself. Though it's hard to reject oneself outright, one's fear of rejection can be reinforced by other people. So I don't do things just for acceptance from other people anymore. I do them to make me happy and then I enjoy it when other people like what I'm doing.

As for fear of heights and sharp objects, I don't think they are part of my reality anymore. I'll have to see for sure, as I haven't been in a position where it has come up yet. It used to be that I didn't like needles. I didn't even like to look at needles. Now, I don't mind getting a shot. I didn't like thinking about a razor cutting me as it reminded me of a sharp object. Now, I can vividly think about it and it doesn't bother me. It's not that I want to get cut but just that I do not have the fear of it now.

Q - Have you been regressed into any other past lives?

A - Yes.

Q - Could you tell me about it?

A - Yes. The other past life I viewed took place in Egypt. I was a young Egyptian girl. My mother didn't look anything like my present mother, but I felt it was the same person in another body, the first instant that I saw her. It turned out she wanted me to take a bath and I didn't want to; she was walking behind me pushing me forward. This was connected with a fear I've had in this lifetime of being manipulated by the women I've been involved with.

Q - Do you know when this occurred?

A - The date I got was 500 B.C.

Q - Do you know your name then?

A - The name that came to mind was Amad, and it was the one I accepted.

Q - Can you describe yourself?

A - I was a small, young girl about eight years old. I had long black hair, olive skin and I was quite thin.

Q - What was the lesson to be learned from that lifetime?

A - The lesson was that, especially once you are an adult, nobody can force you to do something you don't want to do. Others cannot manipulate you as you make your own existence and reality. You are the only one who does. You may think other people are manipulating you but they are not. In a way, I had learned this lesson before that past life regression and this just confirmed it for me. If you're a parent, you should have respect for the desires of your children, and if they resist you, try to understand why.

Q - Can you describe your feelings and any sense you were aware of?

A - I actually felt my mother pushing me. That was very real.

Q - Were you aware of your surroundings?

A - Yes, but not with total vividness. I got the impression of a tiled place and I remember seeing columns. I was focusing more on the confrontation between my mother and myself, not my surroundings. My feelings were basically irritation and annoyance that I was being forced to do something I didn't want to do and that someone would impose their will on me, even my mother.

Q - How well do you think that knowledge is going to benefit you now and in the future?

A - I hope that the fear of being manipulated by women, which has affected my social life, has been overcome. What I have done in the past is to draw women to me and then either they would manipulate me or, from fear, I would totally dominate them. I now believe it is possible to have freedom from manipulation.

Q - Were you conscious during your regression and do you have total recall of the past lives?

A - Yes, totally conscious and I had total recall of everything in my past lives while I was regressed. I was aware of everything happening around me and of Loy directing me. It's just that I could switch my focus from my surroundings to the past life. I was totally in control of myself all the time and in no way felt that I might become lost in the past life. In fact, I probably held on too much and didn't experience as much as I could of it, but that is a function of my conscious which is an asset in some ways and a liability in others.

Interviewer - Thank you, Bob.

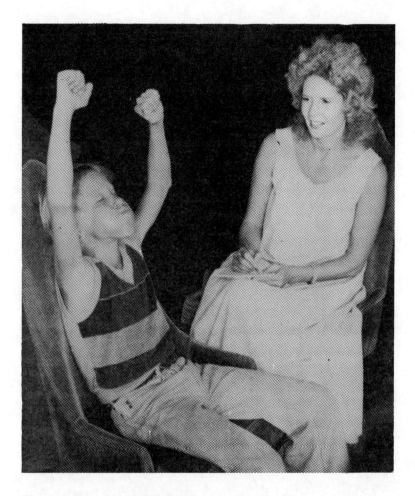

Twelve year old, Eric Patrick handled his fear of swimming after discovering he had drowned in a ski boat accident in 1965.

CAN CHILDREN BE REGRESSED?

Eric Patrick was twelve years old at the time of his regression, and we selected his interview to demonstrate the ease with which children can be regressed into past lives. Usually, they haven't been indoctrinated with "one lifetime" theories so they are quite open to viewing past lives.

Even without regression counseling, children will normally give you all kinds of clues about their former existences. If you just listened and asked them questions, they could probably tell you some very interesting stories.

We have not included all the details concerning Eric's past life such as his name, residence, etc. His parents from that life are still alive and we wouldn't want them finding out about it from a book or from friends who read the information here. That could be a traumatic shock if past life knowledge is not a part of their reality. At this time we have verified the name and the street where he lived but his family from that life no longer resides there. Eric's present life mother intended to visit the city of her son's previous life to do some further verification.

Interview #2

Q - What is your name and where do you live?

A - My name is Eric Patrick and I live in Los Angeles with my Mom, but I have been living in Ohio with my Dad.

Q - How old are you?

A - I'm twelve years old.

Q - Tell me about when you were regressed.

A - Okay. Well, see, I went with my Mom to a lady who was showing Tarot cards. She was showing us how to tell the past and the future right from the pictures on the cards. She said something about death being renewal and it made me think for a couple of days. I wondered about it. In the regression Loy asked me for the thing that interested me most this lifetime, and I told about this. Then she had me look for something earlier than this life that was like those Tarot cards. I was in a big castle with candles all around in Ireland. It was the 1700's. Then she had me describe my body which was 5'8 or 5'9. I had blonde hair, blue eyes, medium build and I was 16. I was looking at a deck of cards. They looked something like the Tarot cards may have been. It was very dark and there were candles and I was studying the pictures and wondering what they meant. My name was Harold O'Donald. It was cold and in the fall and there was a real damp smell. My father was upstairs sleeping; my mother was dead. He had brown hair that is curly and is very good with the sword. When my Mom died she left me those cards, and he forebade me to look at them. Every time he was asleep, I used to get them out and try to figure them out, but I never did. I died in a war in a big fight. It was bad and painful. I got stabbed in the back.

Q - What did you learn that life?

A - I learned not to be afraid. Oh, I think my Father's name was O'Henry and my Mother's name was O'Donald.

Q - How can that life be of value to you in this life?

A - Well, I guess I shouldn't be afraid in this life either.

Q - Were you regressed into any other lifetimes?

A - Well, when I just finished looking at that life in Ireland, suddenly I felt like I was in a car accident. I was sixteen and with my girlfriend named Betty. She was also sixteen. You know what? I've met her on the boardwalk but her name is Joy this time. Anyway, I was somewhere in Michigan with Betty, and we were driving and someone ran a sign and hit us, went directly into us, and then the car behind hit us. We had a spare gas can in the back of the car and it blew up.

Q - Can you recall your name?

A - It was Chuck Farrell. My friends call me Chuckie.

Q - Can you tell me where you live?

A - In Michigan. It was in a small wooden house with white paint and green shutters and a green roof. My Mother keeps the house very clean. She's wholesome and kind. It's got old-fashioned furniture in it. She's 39 and my Father is 47 years old.

Q - Can you describe your Dad?

A - Yeah. He's outgoing, not timid like my Mom. But he's old-fashioned to me.

Q - Can you tell me any of your emotions in that life?

A - Well, it wasn't a real happy life. I mean some parts were okay, but mostly I wasn't real happy.

Q - What about your senses. Were you aware of them?

A - Yeah. When I first started, there was nothing but black for a second. Then you see for a moment; it is kinda like smoke all around you and it kinda goes away. It was a lot like a dream, but when you can feel things, it gets real. I got real hot while we were doing the regression.

Q - Were you under anyone else's control or your own when being regressed?

A - She told me what to do, but I was under my own control.

Q - Was that all of your regressions?

A - No, I got hit in the back of the neck in that car accident, and it kept hurting and wouldn't go away, so Loy had me look at more about it and, you know what? It was another life coming up for me to look at. It was my birth, April 10, 1946 and then suddenly I'm water skiing on a boat. Another boat ran over me, and I drown. That was May 3, 1965. I was nineteen and my name was John. It was along a river, either in Arkansas or Arizona. I think it was Arizona, though. I was 6'2, I had blonde hair, green eyes and broad shoulders.

Q - Do you recall you family's name?

A - Yes. I had a Mother named Janet, a Father named Alfred, and my sister was named Janet after my Mother. She died in the boat accident also. She was driving it when it blew up. I know my last name but Mom and Loy said I couldn't say until we verified it, as my parents in that life are probably still alive and it would be too much of a shock to them. They said that adults have a harder time accepting this than kids, as they have been programmed with too many beliefs. That's why past lives are much easier for us. Loy says kids are much easier to run regressions on than adults, and I know why.

Q - What did you learn in that life?

A - Not to make mistakes. I used to have a very happy life. Me and my friend, Ralph, would go boating every day we could. My wrists were always sore from water skiing. This lifetime I learned to water ski real quick, just got right up, like I always knew how.

Q - Do you want to have any more past life regressions?

A - Sure, then I wouldn't have to go to school to learn everything. I'd just remember like I did water skiing in this life.

Q - Is there anything else you remember?

A - Yeah. Loy had me look at this life and if I chose my Mom and Dad and why. I chose both of them. Mom is supposed to teach me spiritual awareness stuff, and my Dad is supposed to teach me about the wilderness. I like them a lot. She also had me see if there was anything I was supposed to do this lifetime and, sure enough I'm supposed to learn what those Tarot cards really mean this lifetime and I'm supposed to be teaching people about life cycles they go through. And I'm talking out in front of a bunch of people. I guess the rest will come to me later.

Q - Are you interested in verifying your past lives?

A - Not really. They were real to me. It's now that I'm interested in. They just showed me how to make now better. It's sure neat not to be afraid of swimming since the regression though, and I go to the ocean all the time now, since that fear is gone.

Interviewer: Thank you, Eric.

HOW MANY INCARNATIONS ARE THERE?

Duane Leasenby's case was chosen for two reasons. First, it reveals past lives on other planets. This is quite common. In fact, many people who come to us for regressions want to find out what planet they came from, because planet Earth seems somehow strange to them. In addition, Duane has been doing past life regressions for a long time; twenty years to be exact. He has found that he lived hundreds of times before. This coincides with Eastern philosophies which teach that we live about 800 times before we break the birth-death cycle. (Buddha supposedly recounted 550 of his past lives to his followers.) Also, Duane's interview demonstrates the Law of Karma or Cause and Effect. Stated simply, this Law is epitomized in the Biblical passage: "You shall reap whatsoever you shall sow."

Interview #3

Q - What is your name and where do you live?

A - My name is Duane Leasenby and I live in Torrance, California.

Q - It is my understanding that you have been recalling past lives for quite some time. I would like to take up some of the highlights. Is that okay with you?

A - Sure.

Q - What realization have you gotten from viewing your past lives?

A - The big thing is when you recall a past life, you don't worry about dying anymore. You know with certainty you're a spiritual entity, and no one can convince you, or brainwash you differently. Another thing that impressed me was that some emotions that had persisted into this life had another earlier lifetime as its source, and that amazed me. However, when the prior life was located and the emotional upset handled there, I no longer had those emotions bothering me in this lifetime anymore, or that one.

If more people regressed to past lives, it would change society's attitude and help bring about peace on the planet. Also, it would make people more liberal and they would not believe their way was the only way. For instance, they might be staunch Catholics this life and would find that in their past life they might be a Methodist preacher, and maybe several lives ago they were Buddhist.

Q - Do your beliefs differ much this lifetime from previous lifetimes?

A - It's amazing how different my beliefs were from lifetime to lifetime. I find it difficult to even conceive of all the different beliefs I've had; some of them were really strange. For example, for many lifetimes I was a bad guy; like a gun-slinger. Then the next lifetime, I'd be a priest.

Q - During regression, did you ever experience any uncomfortable feeling or pain?

A - Yes, but I also had the pain this lifetime, and when I contacted the source of the pain in another lifetime, it went away. When you realize the pain you have right now in this lifetime can come from an earlier episode, it's quite a revelation.

Q - As you have viewed a lot of past lives now, can you find them by yourself or do you still need someone to guide you?

A - No, I can locate them myself now. When I see another person that looks familiar, I can usually look and see which life and what relationship I had with them, so that takes away the mystery. Also, in the past, I might go somewhere that seemed familiar but that's all the awareness I would have. Now I can go to a place that is familiar and actually see when I was there and in what situation.

Q - Robert Young has said that, "Movies like 'Star Wars' are a lot more real than most people think." Have you ever looked at any lives like that, and if so would you tell me about it?

A - Yes, I can do that. Mostly I did something to someone else or they did something to me. It was like pulling out the lasers and chasing and zapping each other, getting killed and whatever, and occasionally taking off in spaceships and that kind of thing.

Q - Could you give me an actual time or recall one of them?

A - Yes. Loy regressed me and I was in a spaceship and landed in what is now known as Minneapolis. I was implanting or doing something with the population there.

Q - What does implanting mean?

A - Well, that's putting ideas in their heads, something like hypnosis, and that was my thing on that particular mission. And I recalled the area and what I was doing and the spaceship which was a cigar-shaped kind of thing, in that particular time.

Q - Do you remember what time period that was?

A - It was probably about 100,000 years ago, sometime in that area.

Q - Did you view any lives that were on another planet?

A - Lots of them.

Q - What planets do you remember?

A - I touched on Mars, but most of them have been out of this solar system entirely.

Q - What do you remember about Mars?

A - That it was hot and dry. I wasn't looking at the scenery too much. I was viewing what I had done against this person, mainly.

Q - Getting back a little closer to now, have you looked at your past life before this one?

A - Yes. I was in Chicago in my previous life. I was a bootlegger and running booze across Lake Michigan.

Q - When were you born in that life?

A - It was approximately 1898, around the turn of the century. It was the 1920's that I went into bootlegging and things like that. I got killed doing that. It was as good a time as most of them, but it was actually quite a dull life except for the bootlegging.

Q - Have you ever been anything other than American?

A - Sure. Many. One of the most vivid was a German.

Q - Out of the people that you meet today, approximately how many would you say you knew before in a past life?

A - I would say about 30%.

Q - What sense were you most aware of when you recalled a past life?

A - Sight and hearing were most real. And lots of times the pain that I was reviewing in the past life was very real also. I remember once I came to a session with Loy with a real bad pain in my stomach. When being regressed I found myself being stabbed in the stomach with a sword, and I really felt the pain. Finally, after getting all the data concerning the stabbing, the pain went away and I left feeling great.

Q - How many past lives would you say that you have contacted?

A - Hundreds. Not all on this planet. I've been just about everything from high to low, the other sex, and all different races. I've learned a lot of lessons. You sure wouldn't learn much if you just did one thing time after time. One of the most vivid 3-D color ones I remember was in my Amazon days. It was millions of years ago and had big nude girls dancing around. They were doing a fertility ceremony. I was the guest of honor in the pot.

Interviewer: Thank you, Duane.

Louisa Antares, a health food manufacturer from Ohio found she owned
a Southern plantation during the Civil War in her past life regression.

FASCINATION WITH CIVIL WAR
FINALLY EXPLAINED

Louisa Antares is a very pretty young woman of thirty. At the time she was regressed, she was the owner of a health food manufacturing plant.

Louisa was always enormously interested in the Civil War. Yet, she never understood why. In her past life regressing she found the roots of her connection with the Civil War. When people are regressed, it is quite common for them to discover that a strong interest or hobby they have in this life may have occupied an entire lifetime in a previous existence. For example, one man did woodcarving for a hobby. In fact, he said he felt obsessed to do it as often as possible, and he spent evenings and almost every weekend doing woodcarving. In a regression, he found a lifetime where he not only made woodcarvings, but taught the art to his tribesman for over 30 years. Interestingly enough, his woodcarvings in both past and present lives were African in style and methods used. In this life, he had never visited Africa, nor had he studied about that style or technique of woodcarving.

Interview #4

Q - What is your name?

A - My name is Louisa Antares.

Q - Why did you have past life regressions?

A - Well, you might call me a guinea pig or research case. Loy has been regressing people for years, but both she and Robert said some of the methods they had been using could take anywhere from 10-25 hours to get a person to be able to look at their past lives the first time they did it. She also said they were totally opposed to using drugs or putting people into an unconscious trance to get them to look at their former existences any faster. They had always wanted to find a faster method for regressing as many people as possible, as fast as possible. They wanted to do research on people who were not into the spiritual awareness field and didn't know anything about past lives. At that time, I had my own food manufacturing plant and had never been anywhere near this field, so they used me as a research case. After I was regressed the first time, I started finding out why I was here in the first place, and what my purpose was in my life.

Q - Would you describe the actual regression?

A - Well, first we looked at some things in this life and did some drills, so I would have some certainty when I looked at some of my reincarnations. You see, in this life, sometimes I wasn't real certain of myself. Loy said we would have to fix that first, as there was no way that I would have any certainty about times before this life until I had some certainty about this life and would not invalidate everything I looked at. Anyway, we worked on that for awhile, until I felt real good about it.

Then, suddenly, I was looking out through the eyes of a woman about 45 years old living in the deep South at the time Sherman marched into the South. I think I was in South Carolina or that area on a large plantation, one of the largest in the area. I had two boys, quite young, about eight and fifteen by marriage to a first cousin. He was an older man; I had married out of convenience, basically, because there were not very many men or women available for marriage. In time, we grew to love each other very much; I know we had a very good relationship. This came to me all in the same instant. I suddenly saw all these things.

I remembered that Sherman had passed through our farm and, as a collective group, we had fought him off. He and his troops had taken all of our neighbors' food, killed them, and moved on. We thought we were safe, but less than six months later, they returned, starving. We tried to fight them off again, but this time we were unsuccessful. Sherman had us rounded up and locked in the corn shed. For two days he gave us nothing but water and I knew he was deliberating on whether to kill us because our food had literally saved the life of his army. I suddenly knew I was in a fairly enclosed place and could smell corn. I could recall my entire life as a woman in the deep South prior and during the war between the states.

I had been raised on a plantation during the days of slaves and early Western settlers. We had slaves for as long as I could remember. My mother and I were known to go into the fields at noon time and bring cool water from the well near the house to all the workers and slaves in the field. We were all very close and they were more like our children than our slaves. They were very well cared for, and I can't remember my father raising his voice to them. Mom taught the children in a vine-covered shack outside the house. I think she did it so they were able to understand more how to do things and why. A slave saved her life when she had my little sister. She bled so bad that they packed her with a poultice and held her upside down for long periods of time. After two days, she stopped bleeding and then they prayed for another day in thanks for saving her life. During the whole time period the slave had never slept. My dad tried to give her money but she would not take it. She said she really needed something to help her get around and my daddy gave her our best mule and a field cart for her. She slept all that day and when she saw that cart and that mule she just cried.

As I sat in the corn shed, waiting for Sherman to decide, I was reflecting over my life. I saw about six incidents such as above. I remembered that when I was sixteen, and because there were not very many men around, my father asked me if I would marry my cousin, Esriah. He was almost 40 then, but I knew him and my father were very close so I said I would. My sister was much luckier and met a man who had left his family in Pennsylvania and was traveling through our plantation looking for a job. We were both just getting over the fever. So my dad had him help us for almost a month. He was so hard working and good, we were pleased he wanted Cassie for a wife. They were the same age, too.

I came back to the realization of what was happening in the corn bin. We were all waiting there to die because we knew that was what was going to happen. Sherman had been fought off on his way down South (mostly because our slaves fought with us) and now he and his men were starving to death because they had burnt every plantation around us. As a matter of fact, those of our neighbors that did not get killed fighting had starved to death. We would starve to death, too, if they took all our food. I could feel the grief in my face as I talked to my two boys. I told them we were playing a game on the soldiers by hiding from them. I'm sorry now that I didn't tell the truth. I didn't want to have their questions about dying. The next morning a soldier came and said Sherman was afraid it would be hard on us and we'd starve so he was going to shoot us. Less than ten minutes later we were all dead.

Q - Do you remember your name in that life?

A - I think it was Maria.

Q - Can you describe yourself physically in that life?

A - I had dark hair up in a bun. My husband really liked my hair and I wanted to have it cut as lots of the women were having it cut at the time. I was medium built, rather robust. I didn't have any trouble having children and my build didn't perceptibly change from between the time I was a young girl to when I was 43 years old. I was always relatively robust.

Q - How tall were you?

A - I seemed shorter than I am now, I think about 5'1".

Q - What about your senses when you were being regressed?

A - The smell of the farm was one of the first things I recognized. I'll never forget that smell. Besides tobacco and corn, we also had a small cotton crop.

Q - Were you aware of any sense of taste?

A - I didn't have any experience of taste mostly because of the trauma involved in the situation.

Q - What about hearing?

A - I was more tuned to listening to us as a family, to the sounds in the shed, than those outside.

Q - What about your ability to see?

A - The ability to see was just phenomenal. I remember speaking to my husband. I remember looking at him as I was sitting in the corner. I remember that I couldn't feel the rough straw through my skirts—they were so thick. He stooped beside me, and we were having quite a serious conversation.

Q - Were you fully conscious while in the past life?

A - Yes. I was fully conscious. As a matter of fact, I was speaking about it at the time.

Q - So you have total recall of everything that happened?

A - Yes, totally.

Q - How is the lesson you learned from that past life going to help you in this life?

A - That no matter how bad things seem, they may be for the best. That past life made me aware that I was totally able to have a life and make a life for myself and an entire family. I learned that I could go through a learning lesson and evolve to another life and another learning lesson.

Q - How did you feel emotionally in that past life?

A - Well, my husband and I knew what our fate was to be. We had seen friends and neighbors murdered. Every plantation in the area was leveled and the people occupying them killed, so the end was inevitable. In the face of this, the love I felt in that shed was one of the strongest emotions I have ever felt. That was also a part of my lesson, the magnitude of love that can be felt during a trial of life. It was actually a fairly important lesson because my entire family and I had been murdered in that past life which normally would be a very traumatic experience. But the lesson was that sometimes you must do what you have to do and, even though the situation looks really frightful and bad, it actually can bring you the reality of what a challenge a situation like that can be. So I would say the lesson was that you must face all challenges in your life.

Q - What real understanding did you get out of past life regression?

A - That I'm immortal. That I have lived before and I will live again.

Q - You were regressed again. What was the purpose of your regression this time?

A - I have a gentleman friend who told me I gave him a pain in the neck.

Q - So would you say that there was disharmony between the two of you?

A - Yes, and it was unexplained. We both thought it came from one or more past lives.

Q - Can you tell me the incident you became aware of?

A - This was an excellent past life. I was a gorgeous, Greek slave trader, most unique in that my slaves were neither tortured, bullied, beaten or chained so I felt quite the queen of the slave trade. To be one of my slaves was quite an honor and a compliment to one's status in the area. I specialized in beautiful women and finding them good homes.

Q - Now, were you male or female?

A - I was female. I was the only female slave trader in the area.

Q - What was the time period?

A - I don't know. It was before Christ, though.

Q - How old were you?

A - Twenty-six.

Q - What about your senses?

A - I could smell the slaves and hear market sounds going on around me.

Q - Do you get more of an exact location?

A - It felt like I was in Greece. I don't know the exact location.

Q - Where did the gentleman friend come into all this?

A - He was also a slave trader but just as I was a good one, he was one that beat his slaves, put them on the block, tortured them and sold them to anyone who would meet his price. I felt quite superior to him. He was mean, cruel, vindictive and jealous of me. He would like nothing better than to get me away from my bodyguards and had made several attempts. He had threatened me as early as my sixteenth birthday, but my powerful father had given me valuable lessons in self-protection. Mostly, it was easy for me to be safe because my guards were quite faithful. I recalled several incidents of my relationship to the slave trader and it was very challenging. However, he ended up losing everything and at that time I didn't help him in any way. Finally, he was murdered. I could have prevented this.

Q - What was your emotional feeling at that time?

A - One of disgust.

Q - Now, by looking at this situation did it help your understanding of the relationship with your gentleman friend?

A - Well, I learned in the past life that through an incident which I'm not sure of (I think was bad politics), I caused him to lose everything. I had the chance to help in a good way; to move up to a new level of understanding, but I shunned him and this opportunity.

Q - Did you recall any other past lives involving him?

A - Yes, I ran a past life in which I was a woman in a harem. I was not particularly good-looking and I was barren; he was a ruler of a province. This was in Egypt about the time of Christ. He treated me well, but I was not his pet. In fact, I spent most of my time with one of the eunuchs. I remember several times we would lie by the pool and make love. It was very frequent that the surgeons would remove only one testicle of the supposed eunuch, and he was one of those cases.

Q - After you recalled those past lives with your gentleman friend, did your relationship with him improve?

A - Not only did it get better, the pain in his neck went away and after a lifetime in which we were both total enemies, it enables both of us to see our relationship now in a new light.

Q - What lesson did you get out of these lives?

A - That one should help one's fellow man. I wish that I had helped him in those lives. Now, I know that I must help everyone, regardless of who or what they are, because in doing so, I'm helping myself.

Interviewer: Thank you, Louisa.

Long time professional nurse, Doris Williams, finds herself looking out of a man's eyes freezing aboard the Titanic during past life regression.

FEARS DISAPPEAR AFTER
VIEWING PAST LIFE

The case of Doris Williams demonstrates clearly how fears which are rooted in past life experiences can be uncovered and understood in this life.

Interview #5

Q - What is your name and where do you live?

A - My name is Doris Williams and I live in Burbank, California, with my husband, W.K. Williams.

Q - What is your occupation?

A - I've been a professional nurse for many years.

Q - What was your purpose for being regressed into a past life?

A - I've had an abnormal fear of drowning and deep water all my life. Large boats terrified me, and I wanted to find out why. There is nothing in this life that would explain these fears. I've obviously heard about reincarnation for a long time, but being a nurse, I didn't want to be regressed by any method that had to do with drugs or go into an unconscious trance, so it took me a while to find someone that used methods of full wakening consciousness. Finally, I met Loy Young and decided I would see if past lives would have anything to do with these fears. Both Loy and Robert told me that many times when you couldn't find an explanation for something in this lifetime, it could be in another life.

this lifetime, it could be in another life.

Q - Could you describe your regression for me?

A - Yes. Well, first we looked for anything in this lifetime that I might have forgotten that could explain the fears. Finally, when we couldn't, she regressed me to a past life, and suddenly my body started shaking and shivering. I felt like I was freezing to death, and I seemed to be looking out of a man's eyes. I had on dark clothes with a heavy cape around me. I was standing on the rail of a large ship and it was listing very badly, and people were screaming and crying. The life boats were being lowered into the water. It was very dark and there was music. "Nearer My God To Thee" was being played. You know, all this lifetime, whenever I've heard that song, I've gotten so sad and I've never understood why. I was trying to quiet everyone even though I seemed to know it would do no good. And I resigned myself, if it was God's will that I should die, then let it be. I was trying to talk to the others and encourage them to have faith. Some men were being lowered into the boat, although it was mostly women. It felt very strange to be in a man's body. I was very aware of his feelings and his emotions. I was also aware of his smell and the feel of his skin.

The next thing I knew I was freezing in deep water. As Loy guided me, I found the date was April 14, 1912, and I was aboard the Titanic. My name was Mr. Blackwell, and I was originally from England. There was something to do with an incredible loss in that life regarding medicine, but I couldn't get all of it. I seemed to be trying to escape from something.

Q - Could you describe your emotions at that time?

A - I was in an emotional trauma until I decided that God's will be done, and not try to interfere. Then I seemed to be numb and tried to help others.

Q - What about your senses?

A - I was very aware of the cold. I just couldn't stand to hear the song, "Nearer My God To Thee." It just made me sadder. You know, this lifetime, even when I'm a bit upset, I go to the organ and play that song, and I can really have myself a cry. The thing I think I was most aware of was being in a man's body, which is most strange when you are a woman this time. It seemed to give me some new insights into men and I felt it increased my understanding of them a lot more. Even though my husband and I have been married for 40 years, maybe it will help me to relate to him better.

Q - How do you feel this knowledge can help make this life any better or do you believe that?

A - Well, one thing I know is I'm no longer afraid of water or drowning now, and going for a long cruise on a large liner sounds great to me. In fact, I'm trying to talk my husband into taking me on a cruise now. Also, now that reincarnation isn't just something I've read, I'm certainly not afraid of death or dying.

Q - What lesson did you learn from that life?

A - I learned that I would not be able to do everything I wanted in that life. Some things will just have to wait. Instead of demanding things to be done, let God's will be done. I also learned patience.

Q - The Titanic is a famous incident in history. Were you worried about whether it was your imagination or anything?

A - It was too real to be imagination, but I must admit, I ran home as fast as possible to look up the date. I'm sure you can imagine my relief to find the date coincided. Then I could have kicked myself for even doubting.

Q - Did you do any further checking to try to verify the data?

A - Absolutely. I tried and tried to figure out how I could get a hold of a passenger list to see if a Mr. Blackwell was on it. Finally, at the local library in Burbank, there was a very helpful librarian that referred me to a book entitled, "A Night to Remember." As I looked at the pictures, some of the same feelings turned on that I experienced in the regression and my hands started to tremble. It was so emotional to me. Finally, on page 185, I came across the passenger list and the 25th name down of the first class passengers was a Mr. Blackwell. Stephen Weart Blackwell to be exact. I promise you I just knew that was the name. I cried with pure relief because, even when you know something to be true, it's sure nice to get it verified. I couldn't have ever told anyone about the regression if I didn't get some evidence, especially with this being a famous collision. I know you should just believe in yourself, but I like to be sure when I open my mouth.

Q - Did you do any further verification of that life as Mr. Blackwell?

A - Yes. I wrote the Titanic Historical Society in Indian Orchard, Maine. They wrote and told me that there was a Stephen Blackwell and they verified his address in Trenton, New Jersey. I also got a copy of the Daily State Gazette of

Trenton for Tuesday morning, April 16, 1912. It shows a picture of Stephen Weart Blackwell as one of the prominent Trentonians who were passengers on the Titanic.

Q - Were there any other verifications?

A - Yes. There was a big article in the paper about a Titanic Remembrance party that was to be given. So I called Charles R. Sax, President of the Oceanic Navigation Research Society and told him I'd like to go. He asked my why I was interested and I said that I was on the Titanic. He said, "You were on the Titanic! You must have been awfully young." I said, "No, I was in my 40s." Then he said, "Well, you must be awfully old now." I said, "No, I'm only 65." He said, "Well, that needs a little explaining." I told him I was on the Titanic in another life. He said, "Well, I think you and I had better talk." So we met and he invited me to be a guest speaker at their party, at which I saw the huge replica of the Titanic. I saw the place where I was standing when I was regressed. In the regression, I told Loy exactly where I was on the ship. "On the left side, facing the left front. The waters are on the left and the boats that I have hopes of getting in (life rafts) are on my right." When I saw all this (on the replica), I sort of lost control of myself. I was unable to eat dinner. As they started showing the film and showing them getting the life rafts, I saw that these things I had not yet verified were now being shown before my very eyes. I started crying and my husband had to take me home.

So, here we were at the Titanic Remembrance Party and special guest speaker, Doris Williams (whose past life was lost on the Titanic), was unable to speak.

Q - Do you have any general feelings about your regression

experience and its effect upon your life?

A - Yes. I'm a psychiatric nurse and in psychology we're taught
that it isn't what you know that bothers you, it's what you
don't know. This is especially true when you don't know why
you feel a certain way about something that bothers you.
Now, if I had been wealthy, I would have started in
psychoanalysis at age twelve to find out why I could not even
take a drink of water at night, why I had these nightmares
about my little ship sinking. No psychiatrist would ever have
found out why I had this fear. I could have gone to a doctor for
my entire life and the reason for my fear wouldn't have been
found. However, in a few hours, Loy found out why I was
afraid of deep, cold water and why I did not enjoy hearing
"Nearer My God To Thee." It's just as simple as that.

You see, the thing is that I didn't believe in reincarnation.
Then this Titanic experience came up and I was curious enough
to go find out about it. I really got the shock of my life when it
was verified. I'm just getting to the point where I can talk
about it.

Interviewer: Thank you, Doris.

HAVE YOU EVER BEEN A MEMBER
OF THE OPPOSITE SEX?

A Possible Explanation
of Homosexuality

The regression of Doris Williams showed that she was a man in a previous life. Bob Baxter's case, which we will present here is another example of an individual having been a member of the opposite sex in other lives.

In the regressions we've done, people seem to reveal half of their lives as men and half as women. Sometimes, however, they remain one sex for many lives, especially when the lesson they are trying to learn is related to wars.

Many times when an individual has been the same sex for too many life times, the first time over to the other sex, they retain many characteristics of the other sex. For example, if an individual was a man for four straight lifetimes, in the first life as a woman, the woman might look almost like a man with heavy shoulders, mustache and have mannish manners. The same holds true if the individual had been a woman for several lifetimes. In the first lifetime as a man, the man might look very feminine and have many feminine traits. It's just a transition period and the next lifetime will be quite normal.

Interview #6

Q - Can you tell me your name?

A - My name is Robert John Baxter.

Q - Why did you decide to have a past life regression?

A - We were searching for the root of my insecurity. That was the basic reason.

Q - What feelings were carried over from past lives into this life?

A - Well, I've had the feeling of liking tight-collared clothing, and the feeling of being watched. Also, I know when I used to fight I would always go for the neck.

Q - Where was this past life to which you regressed?

A - In Cambly. When checking it out, it was spelled Camberly. It was in the south of England, near Bagshot, in the year of 1620.

Q - Could you describe yourself in that past life?

A - I was a girl about twenty-six or twenty-seven years of age, 5'6", long brown hair, blue eyes and I had a male child of about eight. I was wearing a white shawl, white pinafore, three-quarter length sleeves, blouse with low bodice, full-length skirt, dark green bonnet on my head. My name was Heather. That's exact.

Q - What was the situation?

A - As Heather, I lived in the woods out on an estate. I was married to a woodcutter who had a beard. One day as I carried a bucket of water, I had the feeling I was being watched and kept looking around at the trees, although I couldn't see anything. Then, all of a sudden, some bandit came out of the woods, grabbed me and threw me down on the ground, choked me into submission and raped me.

Q - Did you actually experience those feelings as you were being regressed?

A - Yes, as he threw me to the ground and choked me into submission, that was it; there was no more feeling after that.

Q - Did you feel the choking?

A - Yes. I don't think there was a lot of fighting.

Q - Were you really there reliving the incident?

A - Well, I will say this. At first, I thought I was just putting on an act, but after the next couple of times, I got a stronger sense of past life incidents.

Q - What sense were you aware of? Any visual impressions?

A - I got the impression of the child, and also an impression of the house, with chickens running around the yard, and of being choked.

Q - What were your emotions at that time?

A - Detachment.

Q - Were you conscious while you were looking in the past life?

A - Yes, I was.

Q - Did you recall everything during and after the regression?

A - I think I recall more afterwards than while I was in it. It became even more vivid afterwards.

Q - What understanding are you getting from that past life?

A - A particular understanding of the pain that can be endured by women.

Q - Were you surprised you were a woman in your past life?

A - Not really.

Q - Do you have more understanding of women now?

A - The understanding of women is quite a lot, unfortunately or fortunately, depending on how you look at it.

Q - Can you tell us about another past life?

A - Another past life I went through, I was a little boy, twelve years of age. My name was Phillip Dejarne and I was from the village of Montague in Canada. It was on Prince Edward Island, when I checked it out. Phillip was living in a village that was being ravished by the plague. When I first saw him, I was in the village surrounded by trees, and I was afraid of being alone. Then I went into the village. I was still alone because there was no one alive. In fact, there were lots of dead people around, and a lot of rats running around. They set fire to the houses and Phillip was in the house. What Phillip experienced was flame and smoke and all the things that come with fire.

Q - Did you really experience the fire?

A - Yes, I did and it was hot. Another thing about Phillip, I was wearing, at this time, some kind of shorts and a white shirt. My father was a sea captain on a trawler or something. My mother was dead. All of these are significant as Phillip was very much afraid of being alone, and with his mother dead and his father out to sea, this just amplified these feelings. These are feelings that I experience, in somewhat contradictory manner, even today.

Q - What senses did you experience?

A - The heat and the fear of the flames. That was more than anything. I experienced the heat so intensely, I could hardly sit in the chair while being regressed.

Q - Did you feel any emotions?

A - Loneliness, and one thing I noticed with this young boy (and also a little girl that showed up in the next life) the fear of death to me was not that critical. I am callous. It doesn't bother me. The next life was the little girl. I don't know how old I was, anywhere from six weeks to six months. No name could be given. I was in a crib and I had a fever. I experienced feeling hot one minute and cold the next minute and sickness in the stomach. It just alternated between these feelings to the point where I just died.

Q - What were you aware of at that time?

A - My body was feeling horrible, and my stomach was going from hot to cold.

Q - How was the next life?

A - The last one I experienced, my name was Elizabeth Grantfield. I also got the impression it was Windfield but either one, it doesn't matter. Maybe it could be two names. I wasn't married. This took place in the early 1500's, probably came after the little boy life time. That was the early 1500's, too. It was in England. I was wearing dark clothes with many buttons up the front. Full-length skirt to the floor and a bonnet on my head. As to what I looked like, I couldn't tell you. The visualization was on and off. It was more impression than visualization. Anyway, I was traveling in an open carriage, over a bumpy road. I was quite pregnant, but unmarried, and I had a girlfriend with me who was dressed similarly. While in the carriage, I experienced a miscarriage which turned out to be very, very painful to the point where I almost fell off the chair while being regressed. I was also feeling very sick. The next morning, after regression, I suffered morning sickness.

Q - Has this been occurring again?

A - I think it has just reoccurred once. After the miscarriage, I recalled being in a house or hospital. A group of people came, and were around me, men and women, and a clergyman. They were damning me for being pregnant and being unmarried. I turned around and told them all to go to Hell. I think this is one of the reasons I never cared much for the Church, because I have never liked being interrogated in this life.

Q - What about your emotions?

A - The incident with Elizabeth shows why my social life is restrained right now in the present life. It shows why I feel women should be strong and independent, as I feel both Heather and Elizabeth were pretty strong people. It also shows to me right now in this lifetime, why most of my friends are women. In the case of Elizabeth, a female friend aided her, while the accusations were coming from the community at the time. As I said before, a lot of pain can be endured by women. I think women have the ability to absorb more than men do. I believe that is a scientific fact.

Q - Were you conscious during all of these past life regressions?

A - Yes, I was conscious.

Q - Do you feel it's beneficial to have past life regressions?

A - Yes, I do.

Interviewer: Thank you, Bob.

Successful businessman, Jon Freeman, finds himself as an English
soldier in France during World War I.

DO WE RETURN TO THE SAME FAMILIES?

Jon Freeman is a highly successful businessman in his early 40s. His regression shows that he is with the same family in this life that he was with in previous existences. Furthermore, he is aware of this. In most regressions, people become aware of people they know in this life who they have known before.

In regressing people, we purposely use a method or technique for finding people from previous lives. We do this in the hope that the individual can gain a better understanding of relationships with people in this lifetime. Many people come to be regressed for this very reason. They can't get along with someone or they feel attracted or repulsed and can't figure out what is going on. The situation or relationship is "driving them crazy" or, at least, making them very nervous.

In our personal lives, we have discovered many, many relationships with people with whom we were connected in past lives. In fact, there isn't anyone we've had close relationships with in this lifetime that we haven't known before. It's very seldom that we meet anyone that we don't already know. We seem drawn to these souls again. However, in this lifetime we are friends whereas in the past we may have been sister or brother, parent or child, lover or enemy.

It's as if we were in a series of plays with the same repertory company. The differences between these lifetime dramas is the time period, the props and the character we choose to play. One is reminded of Shakespeare's line about all the world being a stage and the people being merely players. We are, indeed, actors and our roles change from lifetime to lifetime. When viewed in this light, life becomes much more of a game and is not so "dead" serious. Each lifetime, we meet old friends again. We're just wearing different bodies (our current costumes) and playing different roles. *

What seems important is that in this life we have been drawn from one person to another and from one set of circumstances to another, playing out old roles that had ceased long ago but were impinging on this life. This created weird reactions that weren't under our full control. Now that we've had past life regressions and can recognize people from prior existences when we meet them, we're no longer at the effect of the old situation or relationship. It's a much more conscious and causative game, even though we never tell the people where we've known them before.

It's important to know that, in addition to friends, family and enemies reincarnating with each other, we

---

*Author's note:

Here are some examples of "recycled" relationships from my own lifetimes. My mother has been my child in several previous lives. My grandmother in this life has also been her mother and even the aunt has remarked (without knowing why) that sometimes it seems as if I was really her child. This aunt's child has been my mother's child in a prior lifetime. So you can see how complicated things can get if you don't keep each life in its proper place.

-Loy

have found that entire groups sometimes come back in together. The souls are the same, but the roles, bodies, costumes and story lines are changed.

Interview #7

Q - What is your name?

A - Jon Freeman.

Q - Where do you live?

A - Los Angeles.

Q - What is your occupation?

A - Businessman.

Q - Why were you interested in past life regression in the first place?

A - I have always just had the sense of past lives and was curious about it.

Q - Have you ever been to places in this lifetime that seemed familiar?

A - Oh, yeah, lots of them.

Q - Can you tell me a couple?

A - Wyoming and Los Angeles.

Q - Have you met people that are familiar to you?

A - Lots of people.

Q - How did you hear about past life regression?

A - I guess I first became aware of it from the book, <u>The Search for Bridey Murphy</u>.

Q - Have you done any other self-improvement work?

A - You should see my book shelf. I do a lot of reading and I have taken about six or seven seminars of EST, psychocybernetics courses, and the "Touch for Health" course.

Q - This isn't a new field, then.

A - To me? No.

Q - Why did you decide to have a past life regression?

A - There was something I needed to know.

Q - Was there something particular you wanted to overcome?

A - Yeah. It was about my constant lack of confidence, particularly in business situations. It would really come out as guilt feelings. I felt guilty about simple things, such as telling somebody how I enjoyed their company or something like that. I was afraid they would think I had an ulterior motive.

Q - Did you have any sensory impressions during your regression, such as smell or touch, or just impressions?

A - In one, I got it right across the head and once I got shot in the heart. Finally, I got shot in the groin (on two occasions). In Taylor's life it was tremendously hot. I was very, very warm. Extremely hot.

Q - What about tension?

A - There was a lot of tension in my back and the back of my legs, almost constantly.

Q - Were you conscious during the past life regression?

A - Yeah, I would say so.

Q - Would you recommend that others look at their past lives?

A - Sure.

Q - Do you feel that it could be harmful?

A - No, I don't see anything that was harmful.

Q - What would you say would be the purpose in looking into past lives?

A - Well, what I recommend is that everyone has a number one item, maybe it's relationships with people or feeling guilty. Whatever it is. But I think that number one item bothers or keeps them from just being themselves and really enjoying life. I would find it, put a label on it and go after it.

Q - What emotions did you feel when you were being regressed?

A - Emotions are a hard thing for me to express. One time I really felt a strong emotion. It was in this lifetime when I was talking about my little sister. My family wouldn't even talk about her. I really didn't have a recollection of her death or anything, but when I was being regressed, I got tears in my eyes very often. I was very emotional about that.

Q - Do you have any intention of verifying your lives?

A - No.

Q - Why not?

A - It just isn't important to me. How it applies to me now is what matters.

Q - In your first regression, did you remember you name?

A - It was Pete Fitzsimmons.

Q - In what part of the world did you live?

A - London.

Q - Do you remember the year?

A - Yeah, 1917.

Q - Could you describe your house?

A - Yes, it was a plain apartment flat, dark color, dark trim.

Q - What about your mother's and father's names. Were you able to get that?

A - It was Mary and George, as I recall.

Q - Did you have any brothers or sisters?

A - Two brothers.

Q - Can you describe your body?

A - I was 5'10", well-built, brown hair.

Q - Did you see the circumstances of your death?

A - I was a soldier in France. I was surrounded by these Germans. I kept shooting at them but I couldn't ever hit them. I finally tried to surrender but they killed me. I've had some of that dream a lot in this life.

Q - Can you describe your past lives?

A - In the first life, I was killed needlessly in a war at the age of twenty-two while attempting to surrender to the enemy. I was very resentful because in that life I wanted to be a healer or doctor and I wasn't allowed. This led to my not wanting to be in my present life but somehow being forced to incarnate. So I decided not to have any plans or goals in my present life, because I felt it pointless plus feeling very guilty.

The second life that I explored was one in which my name was George Taylor and I was a soldier who was involved in the massacre of Indian women and children and I had the power to prevent it, yet did not. I recalled an earlier time in Taylor's life when I murdered a trapper or mountain man just for the sport of it and got away scot free, so far as the law was concerned, because I was a soldier. I felt very guilty about this. The murder of the Indians took place in early winter, in December. It was interesting for me to note that I have gotten very depressed in December or early winter since I've been an adult. In fact, in December of 1976, I had to take the entire month off and had suicidal thoughts.

Q - What about being regressed in this life concerning your sister?

A - I encountered an experience in my present life that had a strong emotion for me. We were talking about my sister, who had died at the age of eighteen months, and my parents never spoke of her so I did not have a conscious recollection of her death. All I knew was that I loved her very much. While talking about her, I got tears in my eyes and felt very responsible for her death (which was caused by her spine being damaged at birth). The reason for my guilt became clear to me later as I found I did not wish to be born and therefore gave my mother such a difficult childbirth. So when my sister was due to be born, my parents decided to use a specialist instead of a regular G.P. The obstetrician turned out to be incompetent and improperly used forceps in delivering her and damaged her spine which later caused her death. Therefore, my resistance to entering this life had a definite cause and effect on the life of my sister, I believe.

Q - What lessons did you learn in each lifetime?

A - In the life of Pete Fitzsimmons, the young soldier, I gave to myself exactly what I had given to others in the previous life of George Taylor, namely, needless death and having any potential for good taken away from me. Yet, I was reluctant to accept responsibility and was very resentful of my present life.

In the life of George Taylor, my lesson isn't totally clear to me. Yet, I have a sense of a previous life when I was a Judge or judged the acts of others and set penalties for them and should be learning about forgiveness by Taylor's actions.

In my present life, I decided to be very hard on myself and chose many ways to do it. Some examples are: I have in my life, a relative, a business partner and an employee (who was also a victim of Taylor!) who were the soldiers that killed me as Fitzsimmons. I have a business partner, the trapper or mountain man that I murdered as Taylor, and I feel very obligated to him. I could have easily educated myself in my youth to be a doctor or some other type of profession that contributes to the welfare of others, but chose not to.

I gave myself an unhappy childhood and teenage life. I had to work or felt I did from the age of eleven on. I denied myself relationships with people who I enjoyed by refusing to get real close to people in this time.

Time after time, in business and employment situations, I would work at something until it became easy for me. I was successful and had it made. I would then leave that and go on to something more difficult or less prestigious then make a success of that, leave it, and start over again, and on and on—always putting myself in a position of being uncomfortable and feeling incompetent in many business situations. I have made earning a living much more significant or difficult than it really is. I deliberately chose to be a non-participant in many activities that would have been enjoyable, rewarding, and enriching for me.

Q - How can knowing about past lives benefit you?

A - I can change things in this life because I did, in fact, create my circumstances. I always felt powerless to change things or to see that I had built things before. I'm going to open up relationships with people that are good for me. I know that I can get close to people and make a positive difference in their lives. I will also be able to be of benefit to others. My feelings of guilt in business about not pulling my weight in this partnership have disappeared. I feel very much lighter and have a strong sense that this is a game. My business life will be a means to an end, not the end in itself.

Interviewer: Thank you, Jon.

DO WE EVER LIVE
OTHER LIVES SIMULTANEOUSLY?

Minnie Enos is an elementary school teacher. We're including Minnie's regression in this book as it demonstrates three separate lives occurring in the same time period. This may sound unusual, but we have found it quite common in our regressions of people over the years.

Interview #8

Q - What is your name and where do you live?

A - My name is Minnie Enos, and I live in West Los Angeles.

Q - What is your occupation?

A - School teacher.

Q - Can you describe the past lives you just went through?

A - Well, the first one I saw was an officer on a ship. We were in the export and import business and we dealt a lot with tobacco. It was the Edwards Company. This was in 1879. I believe my name at that time was Vince, and I was first mate on the ship, but the company was owned by the family.

Q - Do you know your surname?

A - Edwards.

Q - Can you describe yourself?

A - I had a beard and was fine-looking, rather distinguished. The uniform was of a ship's officer and was black with gold around the wrists, and a white hat with a band.

Q - Can you say how old you are?

A - About forty-two, physically in good condition, average height (about 5'10" or 5'11"), medium build. I wasn't a slight man.

Q - Were you going to America?

A - We went all over.

Q - Can you explain the circumstances in that life?

A - I was very proud. I associated with friends in all walks of life but I had never lived like the other half lived. I mean I never had to struggle for anything. I worked at what I got by directing people. I never did heavy work. I kept the records and all our things running smoothly.

Q - What happened? Was there a crisis at that time?

A - No, that wasn't what happened. I did not spend too much time with my family or children, but they were well taken care of. I told Loy, I guess I had known many women in that life and many ports or whatever. Nothing really distracted or bothered me. It was mostly the business that I was interested in. I could keep it going well with money. My family lived in a plush mansion and had nothing but the best in the social circles. In fact, at social functions you might just be talking to Queen Victoria. There was an Edwards Tobacco Company,

I'm pretty sure, and I think there is even a branch here. I was about eight years old in that lifetime now, when I was sneaking Edwards tobacco and going down into the cellar and smoking.

Q - How do you think this knowledge is going to help you in this life?

A - I think I am developing a more spiritual side.

Q - Do you think past life regression has helped you be more aware?

A - Yes. In that life I wasn't very religious, but I know I was honest. I was a kind of smooth character, and my partner was like that also. He had a Welsh name. We were really slick dealers and never let anybody know our emotions. We were not excitable people and we were not very well educated, but well versed in the things we needed to know. You know, I came into this life wanting the best for myself and have had an extreme interest (which is very unusual for an American) in the royalty in England. I used to keep scrap books when I was eight or nine years old and people were astounded that I would keep a scrap book of the Kings and Queens of Europe. I still have the scrap book. I even sent letters to Queen Elizabeth. Oh, I read every book there was on Queen Elizabeth, and all the royal families, everywhere, especially England.

Q - Let me ask you a few questions about when you were in Oregon. What was the political scene?

A - Something about the Indians and the French. There were some problems. The Indians were getting a bad deal and I felt sorry for them and wished I could do more, although I never really got involved. I was always looking out from a porthole. I was always on the inside looking out.

Q - Was there someone in that life that you know in this life?

A - One of the guys that was a mate on the ship. He was on the ship but didn't dress in the regular uniform. He did a lot of heavy work. He was a happy character and I loved to talk to him. He was English and I came to find out it was Ross in this lifetime. He worked on that ship.

Q - How is your relationship with Ross in this present life?

A - Good. We've stayed together longer than a lot of marriages. We have known each other for five years. I was attracted to Ross immediately when I first saw him on the sidewalk. I was in downtown Los Angeles, on Alvarado and Seventh, outside an old apartment building. I had gone with someone who was subleasing his apartment and I looked over and saw Ross standing there. I was immediately attracted to him. He was talking to a lady with no teeth. She had a wagon. Ross was just eating a piece of bread or something. I went over and talked to him and he gave me his phone number and I gave him mine. The guy I had a date with was just staring.

Q - Do you remember your wife and child's name in that other lifetime?

A - Oh, gee. Linda and Michael.

Q - Can you describe the dress at that time?

A - They were floor-length dresses and just about as many

petticoats as you could wear with a big sash and a parasol matching the dress. Linda's was pretty: white with roses.

Q - How did you die?

A - Gout or something. I didn't die an unnatural death in any of my lives contacted in the regressions.

Q - What senses were you aware of? Were you aware of your vision?

A - Yes, the ocean and ports.

Q - How about taste and could feel things?

A - Taste no, feeling yes. I felt emotional about everything, yet nothing really got to me. I could make things move, but I would do it through other people.

Q - How was your mental attitude?

A - Even. I wasn't rough. I would say I was refined. Nothing could bother me.

Q - Can you describe the next life after that one?

A - I had past lives happening concurrently. They overlapped simultaneously in the same time span, in 1894. There were two other lives as women in that period. I lived as a girl in Ireland just before the turn of the century and immigrated to Chicago with some friends. I was self-supporting and I worked for the theater around props. In this life, too, I love to put on children's plays with props and costumes.

Q - What was your name then?

A - Kathy O'Malley. It could be a maiden or married name. I would say I was middle-aged, approximately my 40s, when I was in America. I was still working. I don't ever remember retiring.

Q - What did you look like physically?

A - I was attractive, a happy and very optimistic, sparkly person. I showed a lot of emotion. I was tall for that time, red-haired, dark red with a happy face. As a girl, I was very religious. I would go to mass, even go alone. My mother took in washing, just struggled to make ends meet. It was very hard in Ireland. I came from a working class family and had to get myself together. I had to go out and make something for myself.

Q - Do you remember when you were a young girl in Ireland?

A - Yes. Just everybody worked. It didn't seem to hurt any as I had a good sense of humor and a good feeling about myself. I was not educated but I learned to read and learned skills which were designing and sewing. They needed seamstresses at that time.

Q - What were the circumstances.

A - I was in America as a seamstress.

Q - Was there a crisis in your life?

A - No. I just made the right decisions. I went to Chicago. Later in that life I lived on the shore of Lake Michigan until late middle age; I would say fifty-five or fifty-eight years old and then I died. My last house was by the lake and I didn't have very many relatives.

Q - What year was this?

A - It was something like 1913.

Q - Did you learn any lessons in that life?

A - I think I learned to enjoy art in the form of design. I learned to enjoy fabric and gained happiness designing something myself.

Q - What did you do in your other simultaneous life?

A - I didn't do anything in that life, except live as a lady. I was happy and loved my children. I was interested in everything, but I had no education to speak of. I just had a husband who worked at a newspaper business and that was what kept the mansion. Everyone was bribed not to touch the mansion during the Civil War. Actually, the Union troops were paid not to touch the mansion.

Q - Do you remember your name?

A - I believe it was Carolyn Brewer of Charlotte, Carolina. In 1869, I went to Missouri, with my husband. My husband then was someone I am presently with as a co-worker at school. The name of the newspaper was something like, The Star. Then we came back to the mansion. Except for that trip, I lived my whole life in that mansion, was born and raised there, then died there.

Q - What does this tell you?

A - Well, in this life I came into it with talents in poetry, art, music, and I think I can draw on these different lives for talents and utilize them. Also, knowing I was both male and female makes sense to me and, in this life, I can draw upon talents that I had both as male and female and put them together and live as an individual. I want to be a person first, in this life, not just a female. I tell people when they ask why I don't marry that I am a person first, then a female. If I can't be free to develop and do what I'm supposed to be here to do, then I won't and haven't married for that reason.

Q - How did you feel about the simultaneous lives?

A - Wonderful and it makes me very happy.

Q - Is there anything else you would care to say?

A - Yes. It makes me feel good knowing my friends are around and some are the same friends from before. I think a lot of them and I have had simultaneous lives and just don't know it. It's like they are still going as if they are in a cloud. They really feel limited as they don't know about these other lives that they can draw talents from.

Q - Did you have to go into an unconscious trance to be able to find these simultaneous lives?

A - No, not at all. You know, I had seen some of this in my dreams before and just didn't know what they were.

Interviewer: Thank you, Minnie.

The notion of simultaneous lives has not been taught so the individuals being regressed didn't understand what they were experiencing and they invalidated it. We certainly didn't understand it either, until we read the famous Seth books by Jane Roberts, especially Adventures in Consciousness and Unknown Reality, where simultaneous lives are thoroughly discussed. Imagine our relief at finding an explanation in the Seth books for a phenomenon we'd been bumping up against for years yet couldn't understand or validate.

We certainly accepted past lives as a fact, but we couldn't reconcile the seeming contradiction in our own personal regressions when simultaneous lives began to appear.*

---

*See interview with Loy for simultaneous lives experiences.

CAN ILLNESS BEGIN IN ANOTHER LIFE?

Through the years, we've had people come to us for past life regressions with every conceivable problem, including illness. Now, we make no promises or guarantees but we're willing to help people find solutions by a spiritual approach.

What we've concluded from our research and personal experience is that in order to achieve balance, a person must work with the emotions, mental attitudes, and spiritual evolution as well as the physical body. We're talking about physical, emotional, mental and spiritual harmony. When only the physical aspect of the person is taken into consideration, it seems the person "appears" to get well but only for awhile, or they might not get well at all. If the other three aspects were not addressed (emotional, mental and spiritual), then the individual gets ill again or gets worse. However, we've found that when all four aspects, physical, emotional, mental and spiritual are in balance, the person not only gets well, but stays well.

This is supported by the comment of a very good friend of ours who is a doctor in an emergency section of a hospital. He observed how astonishing it is to see people come in having barely missed death only to return again to the hospital after experiencing another accident. Obviously, only the physical aspect was treated the first time.

Luckily, health practitioners are recognizing that the patient must be treated as a whole, and holistic health centers are opening up to treat all four aspects of the individual: physical, emotional, mental and spiritual.

Here's an example from our files of a woman who came to us with a physical illness that cleared up when she healed her emotions. She was a fairly successful business woman but used to yell at her workers continually and blamed them for everything. She literally hated just about everyone with whom she worked. She truly felt they were out to destroy her. We were certain that her disposition didn't start in this lifetime. She'd been full of hate for a long time. It turned out that this hatred began many lives ago when she was in a male child's body and her father died, leaving her quite a large landholding to rule.

The child was totally overwhelmed and couldn't cope with the situation at all. Enemies were continually trying to kill the child and take over the throne. This may sound like an old movie on the late, late show, but when the woman found all this out she felt tremendous relief. She suddenly saw her workers as real people and not some imagined enemy. She called a couple of weeks later and said that, to her delight, she liked a lot of people that worked with her. Her emotions were actually healed, and so were the bleeding ulcers she'd had for years.

You wouldn't believe how many married couples we've counseled who get physically ill at the time of a breakup. It seems that if they feel victimized in the relationship, feel overwhelmed and helpless to do anything about it, they get sick. This appears to happen frequently in cases where two people were attracted and married each other in this lifetime but were rivals in another life. This is especially true in situations resulting in the violent death of one of the individuals in the previous life.

Author's personal experience:

In our own case, Robert and I have been together many, many times, truly determined to develop our relationship into a loving and harmonious one. We've been together as husband-wife, mother-child, father-child, business partners, and even deadly foes. As I mentioned previously, at our wedding reception in this life, I became deathly ill. I was ill for a full month afterwards. The illness would probably have lasted longer, but finally I was regressed into a past life to see what was going on. Sure enough, we contacted an earlier life in which we were married and he poisoned me on our wedding night. That was what the wedding reception had restimulated. When I found this out, I got well. I can truly say that Robert and I would not have stayed together if we hadn't looked at our past lives together. In one past life, I was teaching reincarnation but in another country. He was violently opposed to the teaching and had me beheaded. Imagine what can happen in a life if any of this gets unrepressed, so to speak, and comes to the surface when it is restimulated. You may not know but suddenly you get headaches or some other illness which becomes chronic.

We've worked with a lot of people who really look at life negatively. In every case, the negative attitude started first and the physical illness resulted. When we found the lifetimes in which the negative beliefs began, the illness cleared up.

We had one Jewish lady as a client who was really nice and always brought us food, but she had a negative attitude. What's more, she thought she was right, that everything was negative and she was supposed to suffer. She was sure she had been Jewish forever and that suffering was supposed to be her lot in life for some reason. Finally, one day she came to see us for counseling. She was broken-hearted because her son wanted to marry someone who was not of their faith. She thought he was going to ruin her life. Her way of coping with all this was to get really sick and even have a serious heart attack. She was broken-hearted, after all. This really scared her. So even though she felt hesitant, she came to us for regression to handle her illness.

She was amazed to find that she had not been Jewish forever. She contacted several lives in which she never believed she should suffer. It turned out that in another life she and the son and future daughter-in-law had all been together under reverse conditions. In that life, the girl had been Jewish and the mother and son were not. The mother refused to let her son marry a Jewish girl; the boy's heart was broken and he died. Upon discovering this, the mother went home and gave her blessing for the marriage. She even cooked them a huge meal in celebration. Again, a nice bonus was that she had no more heart trouble.

Now, we're not saying that everyone who is ill should run out and have a past life regression. However, if a person is not responding to normal medical treatment nor to psychotherapy, then it's probably time to treat the spiritual aspect. Usually, by the time a sick person has sought a number of cures or remedies with no success, they are pretty desperate. By that time, they've dropped their resistance to look at past lives for the source of their illness. They don't see it as such a strange method after all, when they've already run the gamut of doctors, therapists, surgery, drugs, treaments, special diets, etc., in search of healing.

Almost all the people we've worked with who have been physically ill, have had people in their immediate environment with whom they have relationship problems. They've become overwhelmed by the situation and have fallen ill. When looking for the cause of the illness, we find they have been with these same people in earlier lives in which unfortunately, they never learned how to relate successfully. Something happened in this current life which activated the same feeling they had in the past life. It's just that the previous existence had been blocked from consciousness.

Now, another major spiritual cause of so-called incurable illness that we have found in our research is as follows: The individual has decided, before coming into this incarnation, that this life would be devoted to learning a particular soul lesson. However, the person ended up doing the exact opposite. It seems that if we decide on one lesson or course of action and get off course, our soul or spiritual self tries to remind us of our original plan. After trying to remind us in all kinds of ways and seeing that we still don't "get it," the soul starts using more dramatic means to get the message across. Illness is one of the ways the soul tells us that we need to get back on the path we chose for this lifetime.

Illness, then, can be a blessing in disguise, a wonderful opportunity to return to our life purpose if we will explore the direction that the illness suggests. Usually we see illness as an enemy, however, and we do our best to fight the disease or shut it up with narcotizing drugs. If we would listen to the message it contains, first, and follow its guidance, then the illness would clear up as we got back on course to fulfill our soul's purpose in this life.

Now, lessons contained in an illness can be contracted through some of the newer methods of psychotherapy. But when these methods aren't fully effective because a true connection with the soul or spirit is not consciously achieved, then past life regression might be indicated.

Here is another case which is fairly typical of how regression work is related to looking at the connection between not fulfilling his life's purpose and illness. A man in his early twenties came to see us. He was anxious because he couldn't find what he wanted to do this life. He was preoccupied with his problem morning, noon and night. It was driving him crazy. In his anxiety, he felt he had to do something, but he couldn't figure out what it was for the life of him. Finally, after some searching, we found out what he came into this lifetime to do. He felt some relief, but noticing that all the panic hadn't gone, we looked at a previous life.

He was supposed to learn how to help people. Instead, he volunteered for the armed services, went to war and actually started killing people. He'd gotten repeated messages in dreams and in real life, to get out and help others. Finally, he even got messages to stay in the war but to help the medical doctors. He rejected all of these messages. He enjoyed killing people and actually felt powerful doing it. He contacted a life in which his plane crashed for no apparent reason. He reviewed that life and saw that he did not accomplish what he set out to do and even went directly against his soul's life purpose. He finally understood why he died.

In the next past life, he gave himself an even rougher set of circumstances and gave himself the same lesson again. This wasn't done as punishment but simply a means to learn the lesson about helping others if he was going to expand on his soul's evolutionary path. In that life, he gave himself the task of helping people but also gave himself an incurable illness as a handicap.

No wonder he suffered from anxiety in this life when he couldn't find what he wanted to do. He'd suffered serious consequences in other lives when he'd forgotten his soul's purpose for incarnating and gone off course.

Anyway, those are some of our experiences with past life regression and illness.

Here is a final case study on illness. A gentleman named Simon arrived for counseling. He was contemplating suicide and had an illness that he thought was purely physical. Emotional, mental and spiritual causes had no place in his reality about illness. His mother had died of cancer a few years before and he was in constant verbal battle with his father, although he also loved his father very much. There's a lot of irony in this case. Simon's father is from Austria. When Simon arrived at our door, his father had just spent a great deal of money on Simon and had no more. His father had to leave to go home to make some money, leaving him with us to look after him. However, when I met Simon's father, I instantly recognized him from a former life in which he had saved my life. So I had a chance, in this lifetime, to repay him.

- Loy

SIMON LIND'S PERSONAL TESTIMONY

I am a cancer sufferer and I would like to testify to the benefits in healing from past life regression. I first learned that I had cancer on the 31st of January 1978; although, I intuitively knew I had it when I saw the lump on my neck in October 1977. However, on that day in January (when my suspicion was confirmed), I was reborn. My life changed, and like a young bird tossed out from the nest, I took my first few wingbeats and learned to fly.

In the hospital, they offered me solutions to my illness that, to my mind, were nothing more than death sentences, however well intentioned they might have been. I took that attitude because in December 1975, my mother had died from cancer. She had every conventional treatment that existed. My options were the same, therefore I decided to take my life in my own hands.

I had learned of an unconventional therapy from a friend. It appealed to me aesthetically and intuitively and so on the 16th of February of 1978, I headed for Mexico. After three days on the therapy, my symptoms started to go away, not all at once but one after another. First, the lump on my neck (the only real sign I had to judge my physical improvement on) started to go down. Then the itching, night sweats and the terrible lack of energy quite rapidly disappeared. After three weeks, I moved to Los Angeles and continued to administer the therapy to myself. My weight, which had dropped drastically, returned to normal after about two months.

All this time I was physically improving, but not mentally and emotionally because the therapy only worked on the physical body. I was fighting my father who, at the time, was not in agreement with what I was doing. I would throw a tantrum whenever he suggested I return to the hospital, or brought people to testify to their cures by conventional means.

Then I met Loy and the second rebirth occurred.

Until then, I had believed that all sickness occurred only on a physical plane and that emotional or mental disturbances were due to physical illnesses. From Loy, I learned and came to realize that all disease was due to spiritual disharmony: when the spirit is not allowed free flow through the individual, illness is the result.

I had already realized that my disease was an opportunity to change and I rejoiced. What I didn't know was that I had to change emotionally, mentally and spiritually as well. Throughout my life, I had avoided learning lessons that would have made me a better person. Now, I had been given the ultimate lesson, one I could not ignore. The soul or spirit of man is continually trying to evolve through the individual and when this is not blocked in each successive lifetime, or incarnation, the man will become more and more aware spiritually—becoming one with the spirit... Loy helped me to realize this and showed me ways I could use this awareness constructively for healing myself. I didn't stop using a physical therapy but also started therapies designed for my emotional, mental and spiritual bodies.

When I look back over my life, I can see many places where I have had emotional or mental problems and have ignored them. Now I know they were lessons that I needed to learn in order to keep evolving...

I agreed to do past life regression when I discovered that there were certain problems that I could not find a solution for with the data from this life. Often, we can look back in our childhood and see the root of a problem. For instance, maybe if you were bitten by a dog when very young, when you are older you might have forgotten the incident but have an irrational fear of dogs. In my case, the fears or problems did not have their roots in this life and so it seemed very possible that they lay in some other life.

The following accounts are how past life regression has helped me, and why I believe it will help to bring about peace on this planet. I see every man as a puppet on the end of a thread coming from his spirit. The real man is that spirit but sometimes we become so involved in the play we are acting out that we forget... Past life regression can make us see this and become aware that we have all been other races, creeds and colors and so we can't hate people for those reasons.

I first decided to have a past life regression when certain mental and emotional problems seemed without roots. One of my past lives proved me wrong. I had a fear of taking responsibility and using that as a directive, Loy guided me into a previous past life. In the first past life, I was a soldier in the Crimean War in 1854. I believe myself to have been Hungarian, dark hair and eyes, tall, about 6'6". I was an officer and I had to lead a small group in a skirmish against the enemy. I was uncertain of myself, my men were aware of my lack of confidence and mis-timed the attack. All of my men were killed and I was responsible.

All the memory came through intuitively rather than by intellectual reasoning. That is to say, I felt that I saw, rather than that I actually saw what happened. This was the same for all of my senses. I was a little reserved in my involvement in the past life, so I didn't fully experience on the physical level, but the feelings were unmistakable. I could feel the death and destruction around me. I knew that my men were aware of my uncertainty and fear of responsibility but there was no empathy and they were resigned to their fate.

The lesson I was meant, but failed to learn, was taking responsibility and being certain of my actions. This does not mean that the same thing would not have happened, but I would not have felt the guilt and I could have learned an important lesson. I failed to learn that same lesson in the two other past lives I viewed and that is why I am having to go through it in this life. Now that I know I had that lesson in past incarnations, I am more confident that I will learn this time.

The next past life I contacted took place in front of an audience, so besides being under pressure from myself invalidating the whole thing, I also had to cope with potential stage fright. I was still fully conscious, you know.

The first thing I knew I was standing in front of a cave somewhere in England. I was male, shorter than I am now, perhaps 5'6", with long dirty hair both on my head and face, and wearing animal skins. I knew without actually seeing, that there was a woman inside the cave, my mate. It was cold and bleak outside. I had to get food for the both of us, we hadn't eaten a good meal in weeks. Game was in short supply and I was frightened, scared that I would fail in my responsibility. The wind was blowing and it was very cold. I knew there was only one solution, that was to move further south, and try to find other people who might take us in. I was in a predicament, whether to stay with the security of our cave but perhaps starve or to move south with the chance of being attacked by animals. Again, as in the previous past life, I was indecisive but in this case, I don't remember the consequences.

In another regression, I was directed to find a life that involved my father. I saw myself standing in a seaport somewhere in Spain or Portugal. By my side stood a younger man dressed as I, in the garment of the men of rank, looking not unlike a cavalier. This man was my brother, who in this life, is my father. I estimate the date to be in the 1700's. The time of year, summer. The situation was this: Our mother and father were dead but before they died, I was in charge with the duty of looking after my brother, but now, I had to go away and my brother could not accompany me—I would be unable to keep my promise. I felt I was doing the wrong thing by leaving. I was frightened for my brother's safety, but I seemed to have no choice. I left feeling guilty and irresponsible, knowing in my heart that I might be doing the wrong thing.

It turned out that my fears were justified. On my return, I found that something terrible had happened to my brother. I'm not sure of the exact nature, but it was something awful. I had once again failed to learn the lesson of responsibility and decisiveness, but this time, I'd also sowed the seed of disharmony between my father and myself in this life. I suppose the reason for that is that I love my father very much but I also hate him out of the guilt I felt because I let something terrible happen to him in a previous life. Now that I know one of the reasons for the unhappy relations between us, I can go about changing them.

All the past lives I contacted seemed to have certain things in common: The important one is my failure to learn the lesson of responsibility and self-confidence, making the same lesson appear in other lifetimes. Another is that when regressed with a directive, I reached a point in the lifetime when a crisis or change was about to occur. The last one, I think, is general for everyone being regressed and perhaps shows the knowledge, ability and desire of the inner self to help the outer self become perfect and rise above corporal existence.

My gain from being regressed is an understanding of the immortality of the soul and also knowledge of the reason for the relationship with my father and sister, and the reason for my indecision and fear of responsibility... In general, past life regression has given me more confidence in myself. I feel more in harmony with myself and others. Also my ability to cope with problems is better.

My fourth regression was the most vivid and by far the best in a technical sense. On command from Loy, my first impression or thought that crossed my mind was "maximus" and right afterwards, Roman. I then became aware of being in an arena, my body was physically very big, not tall but very strong. I was dark-haired with dark eyes, dressed in a short skirt and wearing a leather breast plate. The time period was 500, I could not decide whether it was B.C. or A.D. After the regression, I found that the Roman calendar was not based on the birth of Christ and that is why I couldn't decide. The time of year was mid-spring and I knew that I was there to fight.

Facing the entrances into the stadium, was a number of dark wooden doors and iron gates. I had entered through one of them, previously having been in a cell. The reason was I had consorted with one of the Emperor's women and had been found out. Now I must face a death duel. I was aware of my own smell, the sweat of fear and uncertainty... I could tell the arena had had many animals in its day, their smell still permeated the grounds.

The man I was to fight was the best in the land. He chose me to do battle with because of my fame as a great slayer of men. I had been a guard of the Emperor before falling from grace, and never lost a fight—I killed all those who dared to battle with me. I stood there ready, armed only with a trident, and that cold rubbery feeling of uncertainty in my stomach. Across the arena rode my opponent. He was dressed in his armour carrying a mace and a sword by his side. He looked down at me with contempt, confident of victory.

There was no hate, we both knew that this was duty and even though he had the advantage I bore no malice toward him. I looked into his eyes and realized that in this present life he is my sister. Now, I know why the relationship between my sister and myself has always been so full of fights. We like each other very much and even though brothers and sisters always fight, our feuding went on until we were both grown.

To continue with this past life experience, my opponent had now gone to a place about one hundred yards away from where, on command of the Emperor, the battle would commence. He rode toward me at full pelt ready to kill me with the first blow. I managed to get him off his horse and then we fought tooth and nail until finally, as I lay on the ground he delivered the "coup de grace," plunging his sword into my chest. I didn't hate him for it, for if I had won it would have been he lying there and I would be free. I did feel a sort of competitive jealousy, after all it hadn't been my life at stake but my pride, also. In this life I have that same competitive jealousy with my sister.

The lesson I learned in this past life was that even the mightiest can fall, and those that live by the sword die by it. I learned that life and death are not the only, nor even the most important question. It is how one lives and dies, whether one uses the knowledge gained in life wisely. In this life I feel that I'm going to really have a better relationship with my sister, and know that what is more important than making decisions in life, is confidence and certainty in making them. Additionally, in that past life, I went into the fight uncertain of whether I could win so that meant that I was at a psychological disadvantage. I know now that I must be certain when making a decision. If one can just have the confidence and belief in what one does, the outcome is much more likely to be that which one wants.

A final comment; because of the vividness of my fourth regression, it would appear that there is an accumulative effect in doing past life regressions. In other words, the more regressions you have, the more involved you can become, and the more you experience in each successive one. The regressions become more realistic, and invalidating them becomes harder.

CAN WHOLE GROUPS BE REGRESSED?

Primarily, we've done regressions as part of past life counseling. That is, we've helped people overcome some challenge in their lives which they have been unable to resolve. These challenges are usually fears that are unexplainable or have no basis in this lifetime. However, even if this <u>seems</u> the case, before going to an earlier lifetime we always check to see if there isn't something submerged, some forgotten experience from this lifetime. We have done this kind of counseling privately in one-to-one sessions.

Lately, however, we have researched and developed some techniques which allow us to do past life regressions on large groups. We do not do this for counseling purposes but simply to enable people to know more about their birthright and to actually experience their past lives if they wish to do so.

The most common reports we get are that the individual has met someone in this lifetime who seems very familiar or he has been someplace for the first time and has somehow known he's been there before. Here are some experiences reported by people who participated in one of our group regressions.

LARRY WEBER, Carson, California

"During a group past life session by Loy Young I became aware of being a boy about nineteen. It was the early twentieth century around the East Coast of the United States. I was in love and found that my fiancee was about to die. I developed an anxiety about failing to experience sexuality with young girls. She was around fourteen. It was in the fall and I could see and hear well. I heard birds, especially. This fear of death incident was impinging on this lifetime from other lifetimes. I feel more able to handle this now."

DUANE LEAZENBY, Torrance, California

"During a group past life regression, I became aware of having been a magician like Merlin. It was in the early 1400's in about November. I had a conical hat and a robe. I was studying parchments with arcane symbols on them. I was realizing their significance. I was a man of forty-six. There were no other people in the incident but a friend of mine who was a fat friar. This lifetime, I know him as Walle Thomenson who I took a course with in 1957. I tasted bread. It was musty and the fire crackling off to my left and there was wind. I was about 5'10", thin-bearded and dressed in dark-colored robes. I experienced understanding the written word on the parchment."

LOIS WEBER, Carson, California

"I viewed two past lives in a group session. The first one was at the age of ten as an ice skating champion. This was in the early thirties in Maine. I had a slender body and was dressed in a royal blue skating outfit. The time of the year was winter. I was performing on ice for a holiday program in my home town. Most of the people there were friends of my family as well as neighbors and, of course, my family members. Their clothing was mostly red and brown snow jackets with varied colored mittens, scarves and boots. I was enjoying the motion of my body sliding over the ice as I danced and twirled around for everyone to see. The second life was one in Russia around the 1800's. I was a ballerina of twenty-two. I was performing in the Tzar's palace at a December performance. The lights of the stage were bright and I was frightened and yet excited to be performing on the stage at the Tzar's palace. Peoples' outfits were bright and colorful."

HOW DO YOU KNOW
IT'S NOT JUST YOUR IMAGINATION?

Loy gives this example of the difficulty one runs into trying to validate a past life:

Shortly after we married we went to my home town, Quanah, Texas, to meet some of the family and see the farm house where I was raised. Much to my surprise, it was burned down. Then we went on down the road to see the theater where I first modeled in a bathing suit contest. Guess what? The building had been completely torn down and there was a bare lot there. The reason for recounting this experience is to demonstrate that, even though I'm still young, the landmarks from my youth have disappeared. Imagine what it's like trying to verify lifetimes that happened generations ago. You can really invalidate everything you've seen in a past life regression, especially if it was in a city as old buildings are probably torn down and new high rises have replaced them.

Another example of the difficulty of verification is the case of my aunt who is in her sixties. She got ready to go abroad a few years ago and needed a passport. She was told she needed a birth certificate. It turned out that they didn't register girls in Texas until the 1920's.

For the most part, people we have regressed throughout the years are not particularly interested in verifying their past lives. Their main interest is in knowing how the past life experience can aid them in this life. They want to find out what the lessons are from that lifetime and how the knowledge can improve their present life.

The real test, as far as we're concerned, is whether or not the individual still has the same fear or problem they came in with before regression. If the fear is gone, then the past life regression was successful and valid. If the fear is still there, then there is more to look at or it is not valid. It's as simple as that. Here's a common example. A woman came in recently for counseling. She was married, yet hated having sex with her husband. It was a big problem for her. She said she loved him but when they went to have sex, she got the smell of burning flesh associated with death and a sensation of terror in her stomach. We found the past life that explained this. It was in the days of the old West and they had been together in that life. They had died brutally in a fire. She said it certainly felt real and seemed to make perfect sense. She went home to be with her husband and everything went perfectly. She called later to tell the good news. She said, "You know, I don't even care if it was my fantasy. The problem I've had for years is gone."

The reason for telling this is that the question about whether a past life experience is real or fantasy is a common one. We usually ask persons asking this question if they have much certainty in their normal life. If they answer that they do have a lot of certainty, we tell them that in all probability they will be certain of their past lives as well. If they say they aren't very certain in this life, then we tell them they may not be very certain of their past lives either. It all comes down to beliefs and certainty.

We are certain of one thing, almost everyone feels something dramatically during regression, such as physical pain, sadness or happiness, a strong odor or other physical sensation. People always remark about this phenomenon. When clients ask about their regression, "How do I know it wasn't my imagination?" we ask them, "How about the pain, or whatever other sensation or feeling they had? Was that your imagination?" They always say, "Well, no. " We leave them to figure it out on their own. In a few days, we usually get a phone call. Then we're told that the regression experience seemed very real and how much it explains about the present life situation.

Past life regressions are like anything else. When you do it for the first time -- it takes a while to get to it. Then it starts to be very real and familiar. Usually, after the first few times, the individual isn't completely certain. But after that, the question of imagination never arises. They just know that it's real and that's all that matters.

Sometimes, when a person first starts looking at past lives, it's a bit jumbled. Unfortunately, it's very rare that the past lives come in nice, neatly laid out patterns. Often, the lives and times are meshed together. For example, someone was looking at a seventeenth century life and, in the background, there were some people dressed like cavemen. The person couldn't figure it out, but we went on with the regression, anyway, and handled the problem we were dealing with very successfully. There was still no explanation for the cavemen until several regressions later. It turns out that the identity this individual had in the seventeenth century was greatly influenced by the knowledge from the lifetime as a caveman. The puzzle fits together.

We would love to tell you that past lives are laid out all nice and neat in one straight line. So far, however, we haven't found that to be the case. At first, a person gets fragments of the past life. A bit later, all of it will come and the pieces fit together during subsequent regressions.

Then there are always individuals who come

to find a past life in which they were famous. Their current life is usually very empty. No matter what you try to do, those persons are always trying to find the lifetime when they were famous. The problems these people come in with will never get resolved. It's not that they haven't been famous. We all have been famous at least once. Being famous is a very important learning lesson. But individuals who are in search of famous past lives are caught up in the glamour of it and not in the message or lessons they teach. The real question is: "What are you doing with this life THIS time around?" It's the NOW that's important.

Another problem in verifying past lives is that people want to be the "good guy" but never the villain. After a few regressions, when the person's self-confidence has developed and there is more openness to looking at the truth, the first regression will be revisited. It turns out that the person was the villain, not the innocent victim he thought he was. The reverse might be the case as well. The individual who likes to identify with the tough guy will not own up to being a weakling or victim. Later on, they can face the fact of having been victimized. This usually opens up qualities of softness, friendliness and compassion in this lifetime.

We first did past life regressions just to help people find out that they lived before. Then we expanded our techniques to include fears and problems for which the causes could not be found in this lifetime. Within the past two years, we've begun doing regressions to uncover abilities developed in past lives and bring them forward into practical application in the present life.

Robert's personal experience: "I was never trained to do public speaking in this life. So we decided to look first at the lives where I failed at it. Then we looked at lives where I was an excellent lecturer and brought those abilities forward to the present time. That is much easier than going to school or reading volumes on the subject.

Again, the verification is contained in the results. Does the person now have abilities they didn't have before? Or do they now understand the theory which they can then practice and use? It's like riding a bicycle. You never seem to forget how, even if you don't ride for many years. You do have to refresh your memory when you resume the activity, but it doesn't take nearly as long as if you were learning from scratch.

In the past, many people, including us, have invalidated past lives that coincided or overlapped. We thought we had made a mistake. It wasn't until a few years ago that simultaneous lives became accepted. Since then, we've talked to others who do regression work and they've experienced the same phenomenon. They just hadn't figured it out yet.

In all this discussion of verification, we're not saying that an individual should not try to verify past lives. We wanted to point out the problems and the many aspects of past life regression. We've had some people with the money and time to go off in search of their past lives. They've turned up with some really good evidence. Others have taken vacations to places they saw in past life regressions and have been very pleased with what they found. Often, people will come up with names of towns or even countries they've never heard of. They'll go to the library and find in a book exactly what they saw in a past life. Truthfully, we wish more would take the time and trouble to verify their past lives. Later, hopefully, we will have a staff or organization devoted to verification of past lives. The more proof we have, the easier it will be for people to understand and accept reincarnation.

Interviews With The Authors:

**Robert and Loy Young
Answer The Most Frequently
Asked Questions About
Reincarnation and
About Themselves**

The first time Loy Young began teaching reincarnation was over
two thousand years ago in a male Asian body.

INTERVIEW WITH LOY

Q - What is your name?

A - Loy Young.

Q - Where do you live?

A - In Honolulu, Hawaii.

Q - When did you first become interested in past lives?

A - I was in my teens and was reading the works of Plato, Aristotle and Pythagoras. They all believed in former existences. It was like a light bulb went on in my head. I just suddenly knew (or possibly remembered) that I had lived before. I tried to talk to my mother and grandmother about it, but it just wasn't real to them, so I quickly shut up.

Q - When did you first experience past life regression?

A - The very first time I found someone that I knew to do it, it took me about ten minutes to make an appointment. I was in my early twenties.

Q - What were your first lives like?

A - The first one I contacted had to do with recurring dreams that I had in my youth. Also, once when I was a kid there was a movie called, "Alexander's Rag Time Band," that I used to go to when the movies opened and stayed until it closed crying my heart out. It wasn't until I looked at my earlier lives that I found out what this movie restimulated. Also, I was an only child and when I was little, I used to have a little chest full of old clothes and materials. I would play dress up by the hour, always being a person from a country far away, actually acting out my past lives. I used to tell my mother about them and she always thought I had a great imagination. Of course, I soon came to believe that it was my imagination, also. It wasn't that my mother tried to dismiss my recollections. It was just that she didn't know about past lives either. She was raised a very strict Southern Baptist and that's all she knew. It wasn't until I went to college that I met Catholic and Jewish people and members of other religions. I didn't even know they existed except in books.

Q - What did you gain from looking at your past lives?

A - A lot of things. I'm not afraid of death now. One of the biggest things it did for me, however, was to give me the desire to want to make the world a better place. Until then I was really quite selfish and only interested in myself. Probably the most exciting thing it did for me was help me find my purpose for this lifetime. I was actually regressed to the point just before I came into this current life. I found out why I came here this time, what lessons I needed to learn at this period of my evolution. You wouldn't believe the relief I experienced. I did not feel without a choice in the matter, however. I still had free will, power of choice and could change it if I chose to. But it felt so right that I got to work and have been busy ever since.

Needless to say, my whole life changed much for the better. I'm really happy now, knowing that I have a purpose and am working toward it. After my clients have experienced a few past lives, I always try to get them interested in seeing why they came into this life. It makes such a huge difference in someone's life.

Q - Have you ever done the same thing you are doing in this life before?

A - Yes, but I was in a male body in the Asian world. What happened is that Gautama Siddharta, who is commonly known as Buddha, in 166 B.C., made public one of the most priceless secrets of the Brahmans: The Law of Rebirth. Buddha devoted his life to teaching primarily two laws: The Law of Rebirth and The Law of Cause and Effect (Karma) throughout Asia. Then his followers continued to enlighten all others with these lessons throughout Burma, Indo-China, Cambodia, Sumatra, Java, Bali, and Korea. These laws were disseminated throughout Japan and China. Fortunately, I was taught these teachings at that time and then spent the rest of my life helping to spread the word. It was just as hard then as it is now to overcome people's fixed ideas, but it was challenging and rewarding. This lifetime I'm doing similar things. I'm one of the many that are helping to educate the Western world about ancient laws of reincarnation and the laws of cause and effect. We're trying to take it out of the "weirdo" and fanatical camp of ideas and show people that it is a perfectible philosophy. Obviously, we're trying to communicate to the intelligent public because we truly believe that, once the facts are presented to them, they are likely to be open to the possibilities. I believe that there is a good chance of peace once more people accept the laws of reincarnation.

Q - What was the most pleasant life you have ever looked at?

A - I think the most pleasant one was when I found that I came from another planet a long time ago. The planet was Venus. The reason it was so pleasant for me was that I saw clearly that Venus has gone through a similar evolution to ours and had a lot of the same problems we are having today. Yet they ended up with a civilization full of love and harmony. It was a harmonious planet and people actually ended up with peace and harmony. I realized that if they could do it, being so similar to us in an evolutionary cycle, then we could do it, also.

Q - I notice that you seem interested in helping others. Have you always led lives where you were interested in the welfare of others?

A - Hardly. I've been one of the most selfish individuals I can think of and have had to learn just about every lesson regarding selfishness. It's okay with me, as it certainly gives me understanding of all kinds of different people. I certainly don't think I'm better than anyone else. Looking at past lives certainly blew all of my status consciousness. It's a lot easier to help when you've had similar experiences instead of just sitting in some ivory tower tucked away in isolation giving out authoritarian ideas.

Q - Are you ashamed of any of your past lives?

A - No, and I'm not ashamed of anything I've done this lifetime either. I've done a lot of things that I don't care to repeat again, but at least I learned that there are roads I don't need to travel. Feeling ashamed and guilty are feelings that are put way behind you when you learn that there is, for sure, a path to immortality and that you are a traveler on that road. A lot of guilt and shame are caused by going into agreement with people you consider authorities. Based on my research in this area for over a decade now, if someone is trying to make you feel guilty, you can be assured that they did the same in their past, also.

Q - How did you learn to do past life regression?

A - I learned from the same people who did regressions on me. In those days it was real lengthy though, and that method took hours and hours. I know some people using that method who have taken up to 50 hours to contact a past life.

Q - Do you use hypnotism?

A - Well, first, let me clarify hypnotism. It originally meant, "any altered state of consciousness." If you follow that definition, then anything except a pure waking state of consciousness is hypnotism, including meditation and dreaming. However, if you ask most people what they think hypnotism is, they will tell you it's a state in which you become unconscious and are in a trance. From a technical point of view, the zone between waking and sleeping consciousness is the best from which to view past lives. The individual has total control of all faculties as well as full recall. This is also the state where meditation takes place. If we have to identify our method, it could be described as a meditative process in which the individual reaches the inner senses consciously.

Q - Do you use drugs as part of your technique?

A - No, not at all. In fact, if someone uses drugs or alcohol, we ask that a certain time period elapse between the last use and the time of the regression. We want the person to remember past lives totally under their own control and not in an artificially-induced state. That way, they know with some certainty that they did it.

Q - Do people always have certainty of their past lives or do they sometimes think it was just their imagination?

A - Well, each person will have individual reactions. We've found that people who are positive and certain about events in their present lives looked at past lives the same way. Others are not very certain in this life—they are doubters, generally speaking, and so, naturally, they are uncertain when looking at past lives. If possible, I get such people to look at the roots of their uncertainty at their second regression. It almost always comes from a past life. Then when they've handled their uncertainty, they approach the regressions with a whole different attitude and they stop invalidating themselves. You see, it isn't just the past life they invalidate. They invalidate everything they come in contact with in this life, also. It doesn't really make any difference if they believe it or not. The big question is: After the regressions, do they still have the same fears or problems they came in to handle? They can explain the past lives away for awhile, but if the symptoms (fear, life problems, etc.) vanish, then it's pretty hard to explain <u>that</u> away. The beneficial changes in one's life seem to be the real proof anyway.

Q - Could past life regression be harmful to some people?

A - Past life regression would be harmful for anyone who believed it would be harmful. I definitely would not recommend that such people have regressions until they decide to expand their awareness. I would recommend some books and possibly suggest they attend a demonstration to become more familiar with the process. In other words, until they can change their fixed beliefs, I feel they should not have a regression. I believe that circumstances in your outer environment are a result of your thoughts. The outer world is a mirror of your inner mind. If you think negatively, then negative things will happen to you in everyday life. If you think positively, then you are more likely to have positive things happening in your life.

Q - What schooling have you had?

A - I graduated from high school in a small, West Texas town called Quanah. The schooling was basic: reading, writing, arithmetic, sewing and very basic, down-to-earth studies. There was nothing fancy. There was a lot of common sense learning. Things added up, so to speak, and were practically applicable or they were rejected. Then I went away to college. There I was really disillusioned by some of the theories I was presented with: Man was seen as a stimulus-response animal born from mud. There was a lot of theory, but not a lot of common sense and practical applicability. I soon left school and went to find my own answers by traveling throughout the world using direct observation. It was then that I found over two-thirds of the world knew about past lives. At first, I was really infuriated that I hadn't been taught about past lives in school. My husband was even smarter than I was, as far as I was concerned. He left school at fifteen and ran away to sea, traveling all around the world. It's my belief now, after regressing people for over a decade, that you only need to go to school and learn someone else's beliefs until you get your own set of beliefs and knowledge coming through to you from past lives.

Q - Would you recommend past life regression for everyone?

A - I would recommend past life regression for anyone sincerely interested in knowing their true birthright and finding the answers to who they are, where they come from, and why they are here.

Q - Do you find that a lot of people only want to be famous people from the past when you regress them?

A - Sometimes people whose lives are really empty this time will want some status. At first, they try to be famous people in their regressions, but that soon drops away. Most people come in wanting to get better and they are then pretty straight with us.

Q - Can you tell when someone is faking?

A - I would say yes, most of the time. Their aura gets really dirty and their voice vibration is uneven and false. So I just keep working with them and finally, they quit faking. After all, it's not me that gets cheated. It's themselves.

Q - I've heard that there have been many Roman times and many caveman times.

A - That is definitely what we've researched and found to be true. There seems to be cycles of civilizations. We've been around a long time, and our history books don't go back too far.

Q - Do the regressions seem to follow our history books?

A - Well, there seems to be a lot of public relations in our history books and a lot of beliefs someone wants to get across instead of just fact. Also, there seems to be a lot of data omitted and a lot of glamour added.

Q - Do Atlantis and Lemuria exist?

A - Well, I've had a lot of people, including myself, recall past lives in those times. Among these I've regressed, there seem to be a lot of people who were present during the last days of Atlantis. Also, it seems there used to be a much longer time between incarnations, but since about 1850 or so, people are coming back much faster. There seems to be a much better chance of spiritual enlightenment since then.

Q - Do people incarnate into animal bodies?

A - According to our research and the cases we've regressed, the answer is: Not in a long time. It seems that there is a Mineral Kingdom, Vegetable Kingdom, Animal Kingdom, Human Kingdom and Spiritual Kingdom. At the end of big evolutionary cycles, we can pass from one to another, but only at the end of a cycle. It's been a long time since someone was in the Animal Kingdom. Of course, now I am referring to planet Earth. I have had a few people recall lives on other planets and they could take any form they wished and often did so just to experience the feeling of other forms of life.

Q - How do past lives relate to Karma?

A - If, from our present viewpoint, we were bad in our last lifetime, then we have a lot of responsibility in the next lifetime we choose. In other words, you are the effect of what you cause. If you cause good, positive actions, then you will be the effect of good, positive circumstances. If you cause negative actions, then you will be the effect of negative circumstances until you learn whatever the lesson is that you need to learn. Then you change your ways. That may sound rough, but it basically comes down to this: You create whatever you want. If you want to be the effect of a good life, then you create good actions and deeds and you have a good life. Karma has come to mean something bad to most people. They have entirely forgotten that there is good Karma. In other words, it's all up to you.

Q - Do people often come back in the same families?

A - Very definitely. This is most common. Maybe the next time they are the child instead of the father or mother. There are a lot of lessons to learn within families.

Q - Have you personally experienced simultaneous lives?

A - Yes. In one regression, I had gotten vivid impressions of being a lady evangelist who died in 1944. What struck me as strange was that I was born in 1940, four years before my death in that previous life.

That life as an evangelist explained so much for me. I was a very good speaker and a marvelous channel for healing, but my personal life was a shamble. I never did find a love relationship that was satisfactory and my family left a lot to be desired, especially my mother. In this life, I definitely decided to handle both my love relationship and the relationship with my mother before going in front of the public and trying to help people on a mass scale. I am very pleased to have accomplished those goals. I've got a great husband and mother and I are best of friends. In fact, she helped with this book. And my husband and I work harmoniously side by side. I can assure you it took some work because in that last life as a lady evangelist I really botched it. I'm not going to tell you too much about that life as I'm quite sure I still have two children from that life who are still alive plus grandchildren. I can assure you I never taught them anything about past lives. I feel quite sure it would not be in their reality. So that is a case of two lives going on at the same time (a four year overlap).

Robert had a vivid recall of his last life as a German who was killed in Africa during World War II. He got full details including his name, where he lived, etc. Yet, a couple of years later, during another regression, he got a vivid impression of being here in Los Angeles during the same time period. However, he didn't invalidate these impressions, but felt that further research would provide an explanation.

In this lifetime, I'm certain that I've met three of my other simultaneous lives, which we refer to as "counterparts." One (counterpart) is from England and is my present husband. One is from Mexico and he's in the film industry. One is in Peru. If you don't mind, I think you'll find the stories of my meeting my counterparts quite interesting.

Interviewer :   Please, I would like to hear them.

A few years ago I went to Lima, Peru. I arrived in the late afternoon. I was quite tired from all the traveling and I decided to stay in that night and go to sleep. I was in bed sleeping away when at about ten o'clock I woke up and sat straight up in bed like a lightning bolt had hit me. Immediately, I had to get up and get dressed and go downstairs in the hotel to a club show and have dinner. It was the strangest feeling. I felt like I was being driven and it wasn't under my control. I didn't understand what was happening. In fact, the maitre d' came over and brought me a bottle of wine and told me it was from a gentleman across the way.

Thinking it was just a pick-up type action, I declined. In a few minutes the gentleman, whose name was Guiermillo, was standing at my table explaining that he had no idea what was going on but he felt driven to come to that hotel and he hadn't been there in years. He went on to say that this occurred when Peru and Brazil were in the middle of a very good championship soccer game, and he had tried to ignore the impulse to come to the hotel.

Finally, he gave in to the urge and drove here. He said he walked into the hotel and felt led to the dining room where I was. When he saw the back of my head, he knew he had to meet me but didn't have a clue why. Now, this would have seemed a terribly inventive story to me if a similar thing hadn't occurred to me, so I told him what happened to me. We both just looked at each other in shock. Looking back on it, we had almost the same energy and were very similar, not outwardly, but inwardly.

The next day, he took me to some ruins in the South of Peru and started to tell me about some gypsies that had lived there many years past. Much to his amazement, I finished telling him the story about the gypsies. We spent several days trying to figure out where we knew each other but to no avail. Finally, I went off to Buenos Aires and then back to Los Angeles. A few months later, I heard from him and he came to Los Angeles. I knew he was coming before he arrived. I tried to tell him that we had probably known each other before in a previous life, but he was a staunch Catholic and it was just too much for him to accept. Luckily, I didn't know about counterparts at that time or I'm sure I would have told him and totally overwhelmed him. As it was, he couldn't wait to get on the plane when I told him about past lives. It took me many years to learn to talk to people about these things in ways they can accept. In other words, the use of public relations instead of bluntness. Anyway, I feel quite sure Guiermillo was a counterpart. Even though it has been years and there is much distance between us, I can still sense him to this day.

The next counterpart is in Mexico. His first name is Jose Luis. When we met, we had an instant dislike for each other. However, we couldn't stay away from each other. He came to California many times from Mexico City and I flew several times to meet him in Acapulco. He was much older than I. He's another one I overwhelmed with my bluntness. After I had regressed into past lives, I just knew that was why we were so drawn to each other, but he was not ready to accept it either, so we parted ways also. He told me that past lives weren't new and even the Popes knew about them but he just wasn't ready to accept it. Jose Luis is another person I haven't seen in years, but I feel as if there is no time or distance between us.

In the case of my husband, we met and immediately disliked each other. It was like an explosion. We kept running into each other and each time it was like a volcano erupting. For a few years, we kept bumping into each other in various parts of the world: Portugal, Denmark, Spain, and England. It was only when I started counseling Robert on past lives, and we found out we had been together many times working and also been married, that we could finally get together.

Still, after we married, I got violently ill for a month. I had such a reaction! It hasn't been an easy marriage. We seem to know each other totally and what the other will do, constantly. It's like walking around with a mirror image of yourself. We finally discovered we are mirror images of each other and counterparts.

Since we've come upon this discovery, we get along great. It's like we have double the power to get something done. There's no real problem in our relationship anymore. That doesn't mean he's not an individual and I'm not one also, but if you close your eyes and just feel the energy, our energy is almost identical. It's an interesting relationship. There is total trust as we know each other completely and know what we can expect from each other. It's our opinion that teams that are really successful are often also counterparts and just don't know it.

Q - Why would people not want to look at their past lives?

A - Primarily because of their beliefs. Also, sometimes a very painful death is restimulated into this lifetime and they are afraid to relive it.

Q - Do you come into each lifetime with a lesson to learn or a challenge to overcome?

A - Definitely. The lesson and the challenge are things that we have chosen by our own free will. They are there to make us grow and develop, not for punishment.

Q - How often do people find they are another sex in past lives?

A - It always runs about half as a man and half as a woman. Sometimes though, a person might be a man or a woman for many lifetimes in a row and then change to the opposite sex.

Q - Do they actually feel the body in that past life as a member of the opposite sex?

A - Absolutely. I always have them look out through the person's eyes in that life and describe everything to me.

Q - What is the purpose of reincarnation?

A - It's a marvelous opportunity for us to get to do everything we want and to evolve to the degree of perfection we can see at the time. Then of course, there is another plateau of perfection that we become aware of at that time. We get a chance to overcome all the challenges we have set for ourselves on the road from darkness to light, from unreality to reality, ignorance to wisdom, and death to immortality.

Q - Do you ever stop reincarnating?

A - According to the research we've done, the answer is definitely, yes. In the Bible, two examples are given. It was called ascension or the breaking of the life-death cycle. I am referring to Elijah and Jesus. Buddha is another one who ascended and has not taken another body in the physical universe. Supposedly, we evolve to a state of perfection in which we have learned all the lessons we needed and wanted in the areas of physical, emotional, mental and spiritual evolution. Then, we ascend and don't go through the birth-death cycle again. We go on to supposedly much better and bigger games, and we only stay connected with Earth if we wish to help all the other people on Earth to evolve. There are some esoteric books that give all the data concerning these teachings. They are the Alice A. Bailey books published by the Lucis Publishing Company. I would recommend these highly.

Now, as far as personal experience goes, I have regressed three people who were highly evolved as far as I am concerned. That means that in this lifetime they were pretty free from illness, had control of their emotions, and had a really positive attitude or mental belief system, with almost no negativity. In addition to this, they were directly involved in helping make this planet a better place to live and were taking a lot of responsibility. Their family relationships were quite good and they got along well with groups. From their viewpoint, they had learned most of the lessons planet Earth had to offer and they had overcome most of their challenges. Anyway, these three people, after being regressed into past lives, saw into the future and viewed their present lives as their last incarnation. In their future they had ascended. Two of them saw themselves working in another dimension, still connected to planet Earth and helping us here. One actually went into another solar system entirely, one that was much more evolved than ours.

Interviewer :   Thank you, Loy.

In his last incarnation, Robert Young was an arrogant
German tank commander in North Africa.

INTERVIEW WITH ROBERT

Q - What is your name and where do you live?

A - My name is Robert Young and I live in Honolulu, Hawaii with my partner, Loy.

Q - When did you first become aware of past lives in this lifetime?

A - I remember when I was a kid, there was a documentary on British Broadcasting. There was mention of a well-known person in England who, under hypnosis, found he had been a beggar starving to death in Ireland in a past life. I remember distinctly that it stayed with me. I asked a few questions of my family and other adults, but after being told I was stupid and being harrassed, I soon learned to leave the subject alone. Later on in life, I worked on a tanker. One day, as it came into Curacao in the Netherland Antilles, I was looking at a swing bridge which didn't seem to belong there. Then I started looking at the buildings and felt I knew what was on the other side of the channel. It was just as if I'd been there before. I saw images in my mind of pirates in a past life which I tried to shrug off as my imagination. But as the ship went around the bend, I saw that what I had seen in my mind was really there. I had "remembered" it even though I'd never been there before in this lifetime. It was really a strange feeling.

For some reason, I knew this island had an extinct volcanic

crater in the central basin. Even though they had put up big oil refineries, I still recognized it. After checking it out with some townspeople, it turned out I was right.

Q - Did you actually view that past life under regression at a later time?

A - Yes, and it turned out I was a pirate in the early 1800's. I wasn't anything significant, just a deck hand and a drunk.

Q - Have you ever been to other locations that seemed familiar to you in this life and found in regressions that you had actually been there?

A - Yes, as a kid I would go to my grandmother's place in Wales during the summer holidays. We used to go to a place called Mumbles which had a rocky point called Wormshead which jetted out to the Bristol channel.

When I saw it, I started getting images in my mind about a beacon which was used to warn sailing ships coming up the channel about the rocks. However, they put the beacons over on the mainland so the ships would run up on the sand. It was very sticky and as soon as the ships hit, that was it. Then the wreckers would go down and take all the cargo and kill everyone aboard. I found out later in regression that the beach was called the Silk Back and, sure enough, I had been there twice. Once I had been there luring people onto the rocks on the beach. Later I was being lured in myself and got killed. Anyway, I was twelve in this lifetime when these deja vu images came to me and I tried to talk to my father about it. He wouldn't listen at all When I tried to go out there and look some more, my father wouldn't let me go. I totally forgot about it until much later when I was being regressed and it came up again.

Q - Did you have any other experiences like that as a child?

A - Sure. I think all kids do but when they ask their parents, they are told to shut-up. I remember believing Flash Gordon was quite real and telepathy seemed quite natural. However, after being told I had too vivid an imagination, at about age thirteen or fourteen, I just accepted the idea that I was too imaginative and I quit even thinking about these things being real.

Q - When you looked at the past life in Wales, did you get a name?

A - Yes, it was something like Evans or Morgan. Nothing very important. In Wales, Evans and Morgan are very common names. I'd like to think I was a dashing pirate. However, when we contacted that life, I was one of the guys who had the job of building the beacon and later dragging the dead bodies off and burying them or taking them out to the channel and throwing them overboard, depending on the tide. I died early in life of too much bad booze, rotten food and a "social disease." In the next life I was on a sailing ship that was wrecked on the same beach by the next generation of wreckers and I got my throat slit and choked to death on my own blood.

One of the first lessons I got out of looking at past lives was that I had been and done just about everything from being almost as virtuous as a saint to being depraved, degenerated, perverted or psychotic with all the shades of gray in between. I've been both male and female, homosexual, and a member of every race. I've been every color, creed, size, shape and age. I've been rich, poor, powerful, and a cowardly cur who sold my family and friends out to save my own personal lice-ridden skin.

After you realize this, it becomes difficult to be critical of other people and it blows apart any status trip you may have going for yourself.

There's an old saying that what you are critical of in others, you yourself are guilty of. This is very true, especially if you don't limit the time period to one life. Actually, you start realizing what lessons others are going through and this brings about a greater understanding of them.

Q - How do you feel about the sea this time?

A - I have always had a tremendous fascination for the sea. It felt like a totally natural element for me to be in. As a boy, I was always trying to get into boats and had a natural talent for handling them. But it wasn't until later that I started getting more precise information other than a feeling of knowing what to do.

One of the more distinct memories I've had from an earlier life came to me when I was a skipper of a 56-foot Bermuda ketch up in Edinburgh, Scotland. We were out sailing one weekend in mid-summer when the wind totally stopped. Even the smoke from my cigarette went straight up. It was so calm, we just weren't going anywhere. I remembered that there was always a very slight breeze just above the surface of the water due to the difference in temperature, so I leaned over the rail and just put my cigarette above the water surface. Sure enough, there was a slight breeze and the smoke curled forward. The next thing I remembered was that sailing ships of old always used to fly a type of sail called a "water sail." It is a sail that is put under the boom and goes right down to the surface. So I got out our number two set of sails and rigged them this way. Lo and behold, we were making one-half knot, approximately one-half mile an hour. Much later, I was reading a book on old sailing ships and read that they used to do this on the old type of ketch that plied the Baltic Sea.

Another example of receiving abilities from past lives relates to doing art work. Recently, I've been doing all the art work for our promotion. What I do is just open up my feelings and intuition as to how it should be done and I get the overall impressions and concepts of what it should be like. I follow these and the results haven't turned out too badly. Instead of having to learn something from scratch, it's more like brushing up on something you haven't done for a long time. You simply need to get back into practice.

Q - Now, you were a captain for about five years on some large ships. Do you feel all that knowledge of how to handle those ships came from past lives?

A - Well, 3,200 tons isn't very big compared to a 250,000 ton tanker, but let me answer your question this way. Imagine that you used to roller-skate as a kid and then, twenty years later, you decide to try again. At first you're a bit wobbly, but then it starts coming back to you. You practice a little and before long you're doing high speed turns and twists. You knew you had done it before, so the ability was allowed to return. Now, if you had denied to yourself that you'd ever roller-skated and thought you had to learn from scratch, it would be very different for you. You'd doubt whether or not you could do it. You'd lack the confidence. What is commonly called "natural" abilities, talents or gifts are really abilities developed in earlier lives. You simply let them come through without invalidating them.

After I'd been regressed to earlier lives in which I'd had experiences at sea, I started opening up tremendous intuition concerning all aspects of survival at sea. I felt I was being fed the information I needed in order to handle different situations. It was only when I invalidated the information that I got into trouble. I was once regressed by Loy to a lifetime when I was an artist. I had the deliberate intention of getting information about what art really was and I came up with some pretty interesting data. It was very strange indeed, because I felt I was at a lecture with all the concepts being received as tremendous visual impressions. We used a different approach instead of just locating something specific. We tried to tap directly into the storehouse of knowledge by asking for "the artist. I won't get into this too deeply at this time because we're still researching this method and we'll make it available to the public when we complete our testing. When you're doing this kind of research you have to keep a very open mind and not get caught up in your old preconceived ideas about how things "should be." We've had some very interesting phenomena occur when we've regressed people. Loy has covered some of this in her interview. There are so many different avenues of research in this field. I could keep you busy for years. However, our guiding point has been the expansion of abilities and the removal of blocks, helping people handle those things that hold them back both in everyday life and in their spiritual evolution to a higher state of existence. I'm sure that in time we'll come to understand all the phenomena we're researching.

Q - You've had hundreds of hours of regression. How far in the

past have you regressed to? Was it hundreds or thousands of
years?

A - The truth is that I don't know how far back I've gone because
the further back you regress the more you see that what is
real to us on this planet in this universe changes dimension
completely. I can tell you one thing, this is not the first
"space age" on this planet. Probably the real reason for the
success of Star Wars was that it was fact even though the
story was fiction. The whole concept of the movie, the
equipment, even the "Force" were all history. At the
beginning of the film when the space battle wagon had locked
onto the scout ship carrying the Princess and is pulling it
toward the docking hatch, I remember saying "Oh no, not
again," and getting that helpless feeling of knowing the only
way out was in a blaze of glory. Then there was the space
jockey with his fast, armed light freighter that helps in the
rescue. That was all very familiar to me. It was almost like
"old home week." I know some behavioral psychologists will
say it's an attempt to get away from the world of reality into
fantasy. All I can say is that a person who says that, has
never regressed to a life in which his spacecraft was
destroyed by a meteorite nor experienced the unbearable
pain of the crushing and searing heat as his body was charcoal
broiled.

Q - That brings me to the next question. What evidence do you
have that past lives are real?

A - Well, many people have recalled past lives and then actually
verified them. We have many such cases in our own records
and so do others who are working in the field.

I might mention that problems do arise in trying to verify past lives. One problem is finding records from the long distant past. Then there are physical changes; houses get torn down, forests burn to the ground and so forth. Then there's vanity. When people start regression work, no one wants to experience having been a sniveling beggar or whore in some dirty back street. I remember my first regressions: dashing pirates, battle commanders; spice, all nice and glamorous. But the lives I was running were not helping me resolve the problems we were trying to handle. So I had to be honest and confront the past that I was not always a handsome, upright, straight-forward, God-fearing young man. I had, in fact, spent many lives in extremely base existences.

To answer your question, though, let me say this. Yes, people do go out and verify past lives they encounter in regression. These cases have been documented. Yet, to me, the true evidence lies in how past life regression helps individuals resolve problems that they simply couldn't handle in this lifetime.

A therapist who has been working with us and who resolved some of her own problems through past life regression affirmed this from her own experiences. She'd had considerable training in psychology and experienced lots of psychotherapy herself. She had a couple of really stuck spots. But the problems she was trying to handle did not have their source in this lifetime so there was no way she could resolve these problems using traditional psychotherapeutic methods which rely on causes from early childhood.

Also, when abilities start miraculously opening up after you've been regressed, that's all the proof you need. When you experience your past lives in regression, you come to believe it. This happens despite all the prejudice and bigotry that exists in our society and the criticism leveled against reincarnation by people who have a vested interest in keeping the public ignorant about the whole subject. The evidence is to be found in the lives of people who have been properly regressed and shown how to use the experience to improve their lives. I might add here that we don't see regression as a "parlor game" in a class with seances or psychic readings. Rather, we use it as a tool in counseling and helping individuals solve their everyday problems.

Q - I suppose the next question is one that you're asked often. What other groups or doctrines have you been involved in?

A - When you are in this work it's a good idea to look into different aspects of the field so that you don't get fixed on any particular doctrine. The problem with most groups is that they become limited by the reality of the founder or those who interpret the original philosophy. This is especially true of groups that claim to have "the only way." First, it's a downright lie, and second, this attitude reduces the individual's responsibility for his own evolution to higher awareness and spiritual existence. It took me a long time to learn that one lesson.

Q - Did you ever know your wife, Loy, in an earlier life?

A - Yes, but I have a feeling you want me to tell you more than just that. Now, it's not that I don't want the public to know about it, but you know what wives are like. They always want you to show them in a perfect light, particularly redheads like my wife, pure spitfires. You know how straight she is in this lifetime? Well, she used to run one of the hottest cat houses not too many lifetimes ago. What you must remember is that Loy is very good at everything she does, in this lifetime, as well as in the past. I don't remember how many wives I've had in past lives who died under suspicious circumstances whenever Loy arrived on the scene.

It was a big relief in our marriage when we found we'd been together in earlier lives. The first thing it did was blow any pretentiousness either of us had at that time toward each other. Secondly, we were able to locate and resolve difficulties we were having with each other this lifetime. A lot of marriages could be saved if both partners were open to having past life regressions and cleaning up earlier upsets that are continuing into this lifetime. Married couples try to wipe each other out by not realizing that it stems from an earlier incarnation. How many times have you heard, "We still love each other but we just can't seem to get along." Guess what? Their problems are probably not from this lifetime. I've got to laugh. I can see the day when the husband says to his wife, "Listen, woman, what about that time in 1567 when I had to chase off all your lovers?" His wife replies with that centuries-old feminine logic, "Well, that's different."

But joking aside, I think past life regression work done properly, could turn many unhappy marriages into beautiful relationships of co-creation. It would also change the whole concept of marriage considerably, as well as family life in general. Whole families reincarnate back together and are still trying to handle the internal fighting and friction they've carried over the centuries. Here again, with regressions being done, the relationships within the family could change and a team spirit evolve. Get the idea? For instance, the son this time was the father last time, the mother was the daughter. And how many business associates, after many lifetimes, are still trying to put their commercial empire together. How many times have you met someone for the first time and had an instant feeling that you knew all about the person. It's a lot more common than you might suppose.

Q - Now, what happens to people between lifetimes?

A - It's up to each individual. It is not always the same. In my last life I was a German tank commander and very arrogant. I had five tanks under my command at the El Alamein in North Africa. Montgomery's British Army wiped us out. It was about 5:30 A.M., maybe 6:30 A.M. We'd been up since 3:30 and I was sitting in the turret drinking some captured British tea. It was very crisp and cold with the sun just starting to come up. We had already tested our equipment when the order came to advance. In a tank battle like this, you don't sit around. You move and move fast.

We just blasted out of the wadi we'd been hiding in and, at full speed, headed for the British lines. Our orders were to punch a hole straight through them. I could tell how cocky I was. I hadn't even gotten down out of the turret and closed the hatch when it seemed like a whole horizon in front of us just lit up with a tremendous blaze of artillery fire from one horizon to the other. I remember going, "Oh, God, no!" I knew the game was over and I actually decided to go out in a blaze of glory. I just stayed in the turret looking out. It was surely suicide what with all that lethal garbage flying about.

About five minutes later we caught one hell of a shell smack on the nose of the tank and everyone in it just disintegrated. It might even have been a bomb. There was this tremendous sheet of flame and I felt I went flying through the air only it was dark. Suddenly, there was another flash of light and I was looking up at the ceiling of a room. I tried to get up, then I realized I was in a funny little body. I started to cry and a woman came in and picked me up and kissed me. It was my mother in this life.

Loy and I found out that I had deliberately and surprisingly gone straight to England, the winning side in the battle where I'd been killed, and that I had picked poor working class parents because I needed to learn about humility after my arrogant life as a German. The time from my death in battle to making the decision to reincarnate in England was instantaneous in our physical concept of time.

Also, in an earlier death-life cycle, I went to a place I don't think was even in this dimension. It wasn't physical in the sense that we understand physical, but nonetheless, it was very real and practical. First, I went down a tunnel with a white light at the end. I remember being very apprehensive about going into it at first. I knew that when I went down that tunnel I would be leaving all my friends and family behind and would be going out of this world as I knew it. However, as I progressed down the tunnel this feeling left me and I started to feel relaxed, warm and comfortable. The worries and problems I hadn't been able to handle during my life seemed to drop away and didn't seem so important. At the end of the tunnel, there was a right turn. By now the tunnel wasn't physical but the light had become the tunnel and outside the light was no light. As I turned the corner and entered, I had the feeling this was not alien to me but something very familiar. I won't go into this area anymore at this time. It is enough for me to say that from a very detached position, I was able to look over my previous life and other lives and was objectively able to understand what lessons I still had to learn or improve upon. Then I picked a lesson to learn from the next life. I remember actually picking the parents.

Another time I remember staying in this in-between place for a long time, after a really bad lifetime to cool off and get my self-confidence back. It took many hundreds of years in Earth-time.

I would like to end this interview by restating that the real proof of past lives lies within the individual. The whole subject of past lives should be treated as an adventure. There are a lot of unexplainable phenomena and it is a pioneer field in the Western world. The first lesson you learn is not to compromise what is real to you, what is true to your own experience. No matter what external invalidation you are subjected to, take your first step of this adventure and the burdens of life may start to rise from your shoulders and a new dawn of life open up before you.

Interviewer: Thank you, Robert.

BIBLIOGRAPHY

Bailey, Alice A., all twenty-six titles are highly recommended for teachings on the evolution of man, New York, Lucis Publishing Company.

Head, Joseph & Cranston, S. L., <u>Reincarnation: the Phoenix Fire Mystery</u>, New York, Julian Press/Crown Publishers, Inc., 1977.

Kubler-Ross, Elisabeth, <u>On Death and Dying</u>, New York, MacMillan Publishing Company, 1969.

Roberts, Jane, <u>The Seth Material</u>, Englewood Cliffs, N.J., Prentice-Hall, Inc., 1970.

TO OUR READERS

We hope that you've enjoyed our discourse on reincarnation and past lives. We also hope that you found this unique technique of past life regression to be a valuable tool for self-discovery.

Robert and Loy Young, and highly trained members of the Relationship Training Institute, International are available for past life regression seminars and personal counseling. For further information, please write to:

Seminar Coordinator
Relationship Training Institute, International
P. O. Box 27373
Honolulu, Hawaii 96827
Or call (808) 533-6452

OTHER PRODUCTS AND SERVICES
BY THE AUTHORS

Robert and Loy Young are the authors and creators of several publications and audio/video cassette programs that present their Technology of Harmonious Relationships; wonderfully effective ways to improve your life and your relationships with self, family, friends, co-workers and all of humanity. Here is your chance to experience clarity and harmony in your relationships as hundreds have done by following the teachings of these two internationally recognized relationship experts.

PRODUCTS

You and Your Relationship to Dreams
Did you know that the types of dreams you have are accurate indications of your level of spiritual evolution and that you can work on your spiritual evolution while you sleep? Learn to prepare yourself for "night school" and the world of dreams. (audio cassette)

You and Your Relationship to Sex
Here is a vision of how adventurous, alive and passionate relationships can continue to be many years after the first date. You will learn how relationships can really work when we are willing to go beyond the traditional and experience sex on all levels of our existence. (audio cassette)

Legends
Have you ever asked yourself the following questions? "Where did we come from?" "Why are we here?" "Where are we going?" You will find the answers to these eternal questions in a way that neither the Genesis story in the Bible nor Darwin's Theory of Evolution have been able to do. (audio cassette)

After You Die
What happens after death? Is there a Heaven and a Hell, or does it just all end? Get ready for a viewpoint that is both as ancient as the Himalayas and as new as the microcomputer. (audio cassette)

Who Are You?
Ever wonder how some people can have their lives really together in some areas and yet have major problems in others? This program will show you how to bring yourself to your highest state and have a life that really works. (audio cassette)

Evolutionary Chart
(Evolution of Consciousness Through Service to Humanity)
This poster-size (10.5 x 16.5 inches) chart gives you the steps and helps you see just where you are on your evolutionary path.

Monthly Energy Home-Study Course
Here is an opportunity to accelerate your spiritual growth and enrich your life by consciously using the different types of energy of each constellation to acquire specific virtues monthly. This is a series of 12 workbooks accompanied by monthly lectures on audio and video cassettes. The most valuable birthday gift you could give yourself and loved ones. Set of workbook/audio recording or workbook/audio/video recordings.

Everything Is Energy
The basics of Dragon Psychology as a discipline for service to humanity.

SERVICES

<u>Relationships of the Future: A Next-Step Technology of Conflict Prevention.</u> This seminar is designed to teach participants how to recognize and resolve issues that cause conflicts. The emphasis is on prevention rather than mediation or negotiations--conflict resolution methods which are employed <u>after</u> a serious dispute has erupted. The techniques of conflict prevention are taught in weekend, two-week and month-long workshops.

<u>Leadership Through Equality.</u> A new technology of leadership based on equality with equal responsibility. The skills taught are imperative in our age where authority no longer flows from the top down. This experiential seminar is designed for weekends, two-week and one-month sessions.

<u>In-House Seminars.</u> The Harmonious Relationship Technology can be tailored to meet the specific human resource development needs of any organization. Our techniques are highly suited for group retreats.

<u>Consultation Service.</u> For individuals, groups, businesses and government organizations anywhere in the world.

<u>Evolution of Consciousness.</u> This seminar is designed to help you master the Human Kingdom and evolve to the Immortal Kingdom. It answers age-old questions about your relationship to the universe: Who am I? Where do I come from? Why am I here? Where am I going? What do I need to do to get there? Is there an alternative to death? What happenns when I die? Content is designed for weekend, two-week and one-month seminars.

<u>Life Patterns.</u> A weekend seminar based on the concept that your beliefs create your external environment. It is designed to help you handle the negative aspects of your beliefs in order to create harmonious relationships.

WHERE TO GET
MORE INFORMATION
ABOUT OUR PROGRAMS

Your nearest contact:

<u>Hawaii</u>

The Relationship Training Institute Int'l
2036 Pauoa Road
Honolulu, Hawaii 96813
Seminar Information: (808) 533-6452
Program Information: (808) 528-4855
Community Service: (808) 531-6379

Mailing Address:
P. O. Box 27373
Honolulu, Hawaii 96827

<u>Australia</u>

Lewis Farrell
Conscious Technologies Int'l
14-238 The Avenue
Parkville, Victoria 3205
Australia
(Melbourne)

James & Sherrill Lightheart Sellman
Light Unlimited Productions
33 Eastment Street
Rainworth, Queensland 4065
Australia
(Brisbane)

Diane McCann
Lot 2 Main South Road
O'Halloran Hill 5158
South Australia
(Adelaide)

Michael & Quentin Adamedes
Euroa House
236 Darling Street
Balmain 2041
Australia
(Sydney)

Washington, D.C.

Maggie Scobie
Relationship Training Institute
4530 16th Street N.W.
Washington, D.C. 20011

Baltimore, Maryland

Lelia Griswold
Relationship Training Inc.
2836 N. Calvert St.
Baltimore, Maryland 21218